The Joy of Prayer
The Way to Intimacy with God

James E. McReynolds

The Joy of Prayer: The Way to Intimacy with God
ISBN: Softcover 978-1-951472-55-9
Copyright © 2020 by James E. McReynolds

All rights reserved. No part of this book may be reproduced or transmitted in any form or by any means, electronic or mechanical, including photocopying, recording, or by any information storage and retrieval system, without permission in writing from the publisher.

www.parsonsporch.com

The Joy of Prayer
The Way to Intimacy with God

Keep watch, dear Lord, with those who work, or watch, or weep, bless the dying, soothe the suffering, pity the afflicted, shield the joyous for your love's sake. Amen.

~-Saint Augustine

Dedication

To all those with whom I have worshiped and prayed in the Kingdom of God on earth and in heaven.

Contents

Dedication 7
Foreword 11
Introduction 15
Chapter One 23
  Enjoying God
Chapter Two 31
  Sharing God's Dream
Chapter Three 39
  The Joy of Answered Prayer
Chapter Four 48
  Going on in Intimacy with God
Chapter Five 59
  The Joy of Praying with Others
Chapter Six 66
  Incomparable Benefits of Prayer
Chapter Seven 75
  Praying for Forgiveness Brings Healing
Chapter Eight 87
  Discovering Our Calling in Intimate Prayer
Chapter Nine 95
  Prayer and the Joy of Sensuality
Chapter Ten 103
  Prayer as a Healing Word
Bibliography 114
About the Author 118

I have experienced union with the eternal. And so, I possess a heart which secures me from dying of thirst in the desert of life.

~Albert Schweitzer

Foreword

Dr. John Killinger

As I was reading the manuscript of this book, *The Joy of Prayer: The Way to Intimacy with God*, I had an epiphany. I mean a real one. I actually had the sense of being in the presence of God. I felt closer to God than I had ever felt while reading a book, even the Bible itself.

And the feeling lingered for hours and days.

I know this a very extravagant statement, but it is true. I do not normally say something like this about a book I am reading or reviewing, and all my friends know that.

The Joy of Prayer has given me insights into the gift of prayer that I never had before, even when reading the works of such popular writers as Thomas Merton, Anne Lamott, and Harry Emerson Fosdick.

The reason undoubtedly lies in the unique life and personality and point of view of the author of *The Joy of Prayer*, the Rev. Dr. James E. McReynolds.

I have known Jim for more than 40 years—ever since I was his major professor in the doctoral program at Vanderbilt University. Jim was serving at the Sunday School Board of the Southern Baptist Convention, located a few blocks from the Vanderbilt campus.

I liked Jim from the first. He has always been a modest, sweet-spirited man, who loves God as much as any other person.

It was some years after Jim completed his work at Vanderbilt, he participated in a seminar with the famous Norman Vincent

Peale, author of *The Power of Positive Thinking*. Peale's School of Practical Christianity was held in Pawling, New York, a few miles from the city where his pastorate, Marble Collegiate Church was located. Peale noticed how effectively and passionately Jim talked about joy in a sermon he preached there. Peale then anointed Jim as the Minister of Joy to the World as a tribute to his incredible unique style of communicating.

This apparently clarified Jim's thinking about joy and his life's calling, because ever since that day, in sermons and books, he has always headed cross- country and into places throughout the world and without hesitation he shared the wonderful subject of joy.

The Joy of Prayer, I believe, is the finest book he has written. This is why I felt an epiphany while I was reading it. His writing is so transparent to Jim's own devotionalism and sensitivity as a pastor—and to the God in whose presence Jim delights with intimate prayers.

Jim has a subtle way of talking about praying from his heart of hearts. For him, it's not an academic subject. It is the revelation of who he is and how he has lived his life in the transforming presence of the Divine Being.

His book is full of little asides, small references to things thought or said, that illumine the subject of prayer with soft, fresh light, so that the reader thinks, "Hey, that's so beautiful. I never thought of that before. And it is so revealing!"

As a friend and devotee of Jim, I was especially moved by brief mentions of his own personal life as a Christian and as a minister, like his memory of playing with his little daughter Linda when he was putting her to bed. "Often, I brushed my hand across her face, kissed her on the cheek, and told her how much I loved her. Bedtime was an opportunity for me to be with her in a special way. Her books were put back on the shelves, toys were put away, and in that silence, we felt the power when we told each other that we felt the warmth of love. I shall never forget when she gazed into my eyes and quietly and lovingly just said, 'Daddy.'"

That's the author of this book at his best, when, without even meaning to or trying, he reveals the quiet, loving manner of his spiritual being, something that he has acquired through lifelong intimacy with God. Intimacy.

That's what this book is about.

Intimacy with God through prayer and quiet devotion. Who does not want it? Who isn't changed by it?

I won't be surprised to learn that many other readers have an experience similar to my own as they read this book. It is a rich and rare experience, and I know you will recognize it when it happens to you.

Introduction

Are you enjoying an intimacy with God? The Westminster Confession of Faith stated, "(Humankind's) chief purpose is to glorify God and enjoy God forever. Prayer is not a remedy. Praying becomes a living relationship with the living God. Sharing the whole of our soul is tough work. All of us struggle with prayer. We want God to be closer, to be an intimate companion, who is always present in our lives. We want to be silent with God and knowing God with all our senses. I wondered if God was longing for me. I want to share with you how my own understanding, experience, and practice of prayer have expanded. I have enjoyed bringing all I am, and all I am becoming in relationship with God. I pray with my body and soul and my journey never stops. I pray this book will stir the fires of your own desire for God, encourage you in your own searching.

In my earlier book, *The Joy of Spirituality*, I shared ways of relating to God. And prayer is at the heart of that deepening and growing relationship. My images of God have changed as the God who is "within me" helps me to know myself as God has known me before my birth. As I observe God in friends and family, I am guided into right relationships with all those I encounter. As I see God in Jesus, I find a clearer relationship with him. As I accept these new images, I will learn more about being intimate with God. I believe God loved me before I loved God. When I anticipate praying with God, I had to begin somewhere just as Jesus' disciples asked questions about how to pray. God wants to be in relationship with me. God knows what I need and who I am. The more of myself I bring, the more joy I experience. I bring all my own emotions, intuitions, imaginations, surrendering to all of who I am and all of whom God is. My lifelong friend Dr. John Killinger said of his writing his book, *Bread for the Wilderness, Wine for the Journey*, "I knew I had to write a book on prayer, if for no other reason than to sort out my feelings and beliefs on the subject." See page 16 of his 1976 book. This work is a must read for a student of prayer. I have a whole shelf in my home library of his published books.

One of the difficult factors in writing a book on prayer is that each person's experience is unique. No two people pray in the same way. No two people have identical experiences of God. No two people have the same gifts with words. None of us have the same disposition toward silence. Generalizations concerning prayer are impossible. We come into God's presence alone. We bring all our graces and our sins. God takes us as we are, loving us as a special child.

Prayer can be private or public. It can be verbal or silent. Prayer embraces all creation as we try to respond to a God who continually bless us and calls us to Ike God's image. Our brief life journey gives us an opportunity to serve and pray.

Prayer is an adventurous journey of opening up God's surprises, including God's love. I have experienced a depth in my soul in breathtaking intimacy with God's presence. This loving presence transfigures us into God's dream for our wholeness and healing of our brokenness.

As one gets father from this connection with the love of God, human imagination cannot envision prayer's power, availability, nor its unique sharing nature. People keep on being hurried, busy, and living with so many troubles and earthly trivialities we lose sight of God's dreams. We miss out on so much love and joy that can come into life. To be loved is the most essential need. Some try to be perfect to earn love. Others repress this yearning and have a vague restlessness. They continue to be hungrier and emptier deep inside. Love just becomes more elusive.

The purpose of my attempts to bring joy to the world by sharing some light on the joy of connecting with God in prayer. What a joy to be loved by God just as I am. The experience of being loved by God becomes the reason is impossible for us to separate loving God from loving others. We are most near to God when we begin to love. My own attempts have included stillness and silence, imagination and movement, play, and work. To this day, my longings and hunger have not been fully satisfied. Still I walk with God in my life's pathway and my journey will never cease. My humble ministry holds the purpose of encouraging my readers in their own yearnings toward God and searching with you in your ways of processing these ways to enjoy intimacy with God. I have read volumes of books by Buttrick, Fosdick, Foster, Killinger, and others, including those who have participated in my Vision Quests for Joy in prayer retreats that enabled my own vision of God. I pray my sharing while praying with the Holy Spirit will help my readers can know and share their own vision.

The integration and synthesis of the student always differs from that of the teacher, parishioner, friends, or family, because it has the unique element of personal experience.

During the College World Series in Omaha for more than 20 years, the College World Series Ministry has been graciously done for baseball fans and the players from the eight teams who are honored to play. This includes instruction by major leaguers, college stars, banquets, prayer, and Bible study in the hotels where the young men live. June is a hot time in Nebraska. As part of this ministry, volunteers give bottles of cold water to those in the stands. On each bottle there is a label that reads, "Everyone who drinks this water will be thirsty again. But whoever drinks the water I give him will never be thirsty; no, the water I give shall become a fountain within him, leaping up to provide eternal life." John 4:13-14.

We live in a world where people have never walked through with so much fear, anxiety, and scarcity. People are bombarded with self-preservation. There have been times for me when my spiritual well runs dry. For me and for you, the image of God changes That's the stage when we are tempted to abandon prayer.

Read I Kings 19:9-12.

Elijah discovered that God was not in the wind or the earthquake or the fire, but in a whispering silence. God initiates our encounters. God determines when, how, and where we will experience the connection. There are times when God feels close, and times when God feels far away. Prayer celebrating the joys can be rare. We discover the love of God in the drought of the dark nights of the soul. Be patient. God is. The water of life will flow again. We will realize the meaning and the joy of prayer as an encounter with God in love. The Lord works gradually and never tests us beyond our strength. Early in our prayer life there comes times of dryness that is prolonged. This experience makes us feel that is absent. This is what Jesus felt at the cross as he "learned obedience through suffering." This enables our passion for God's will, as Jesus came to experience.

There is joy in the stillness in the presence, just as good friends find joy simply in being together. The hard labor of getting to know God bears fruit in the joy of being with God. As our prayer moves from knowing to loving, the focus shifts, because it is the will that loves. The joy of experiencing God in prayer is not an end in itself, but it is the path that we walk as our virtues are strengthened. These virtues and the fruit of the Spirit become more and more rooted in us.

I find myself filled with both joy and apprehension because I know myself enough to doubt that I had even the remote possibility of living worthy of God's love. I cannot respond adequately to the love of God. Nobody ever does.

In our prayer life, we become more and more aware of being the clay in the hands of the potter. The clay does nothing to enable it to create beauty, but it is sensitive to the potter's touch. The clay is never broken by anything the potter does with it. Sometimes we like the clay become rigid, selfish, greedy, and in danger of breaking. Read Jeremiah 18:1-6. Sin has misshapen us, so the image of God in us is deformed and ugly. Out of this reality, we actually want to be broken because our desire is to be like God. Nobody comes to this moment of desire to be like God quickly. This desire comes after years of purifying prayer in the lives of those who prayer faithfully. If we do not develop in love, it is not because God's love is limited. I have been privileged to celebrate the marriages of hundreds of couples who sincerely say they are called to love each other "for better or worse." Some do not realize what they are promising. When the "worse" comes as it always will, they are saying they will attempt to survive anything with the grace of God. Hard times, war, and deadly diseases are not obstacles to the growth of love.

In the times of darkness, we begin to realize that darkness is light. The potter is giving us eyes to see, gratitude for those trials which caused us misery that fashioned us into resurrection people. "I wish for you my friend the happiness that I've found." Like the writer of I John 1:4 said, "Our purpose in writing you this is that our joy may be complete."

We become clay in the hands of the potter. In those dark nights of the soul, everything is totally beyond our capacities. Our hearts are mysteriously stretched so we can hold and trust the infinite love. We are at home in the dark, because, in faith we are assured that the potter is shaping the clay, even though the clay is unaware of the work taking place. Our experience of darkness is the only sure way to the eternal vision that we desire. God is creating a soul to last for eternity in the Next Place.

In a year's preparation for this writing, I read volumes including two out of print books: *Prayer* written by George A. Buttrick and *The Meaning of Prayer* by Harry Emerson Fosdick. Buttrick's book is quite scholarly. I took courses from him at Vanderbilt University Divinity School. I took a course on Fosdick at Vanderbilt. Both books have been helpful, but most people with whom I have prayed with, counseled in private, or preached sermons on prayer prefer more simplicity, more of the difficulties yet importance of praying. Both authors served as pastors of local congregations in New York City.

I have spent many hours reading through the works scholars of these times had read. They used works such as Samuel McComb's *Prayer: What It Does and What It Is*, Forsythe and Greenwell's *The Power of Prayer*, Anna Louise Strong, *The Psychology of Prayer*, *The Prayers of the Bible* by John Edgar McFadyen, *The Doctrine of Prayer* by James Freeman, *The Double Search* by Rufus M. Jones, *The Place of Prayer in the Christian Religion* by James Campbell, *Communion With God* by Wilhelm Herrman, *With Christ in the School of Prayer* by Andrew Murray, *Prayers of the Social Awakening* by Walter Rauschenbusch, *A Book of Public Prayer* by Henry Ward Beecher.

I found these in the library at Yale University Divinity School. I suspect that I have written and published more books on joy than any other person in the world. Writing *the Joy of Prayer* is a summation of my yearning to be intimate and to share the joy of the Lord as my strength. Mother Teresa said, "Listen in silence because if your heart is full of other things, you cannot hear the voice of God." Elijah heard God say, "*Kol demama daka*," meaning "the sound of thin silence." Quieting the world brings enjoyment of God. It is an intimate feeling. Imagine you are in the place that makes you feel the highest happiness in all the world. Imagine you are with the person you love most. Imagine the deep peace.

God never contradicts the living Word. Keep listening.

The desire is thy prayers; and if thy desire is without ceasing, thy prayer will also be without ceasing. The continuance of your longing is the continuance of your prayer.

~Unknown

Chapter One

Enjoying God

When my daughter Linda was born, I went to look at her in the nursery at Nashville Memorial Hospital. As I looked at her, something opened deep within me. I had not experienced the intimacy and love a father, but that day I was aware of the Father within me working through me to be my daughter's daddy. There was a joy that awakened me in a deep and tender love that I had never experienced. Through this love, I knew and accepted the love of God for me and all God's children.

God is love and God loves all people. During times of war, pandemics, and other unfortunate events, our life experiences are painful. As these worst of times come our way, we do not feel or believe that there is a loving fatherly presence in the world. They think their faith failed them terribly. Living through the shocking and unbelievable times leads to the conclusion that the earth is dangerous and deadly deviant. Jesus gives us assures us that we have an invisible support. In spite of appearances and experiences, God continues to be present. Prayer is a lifestyle when intimacy with Jesus is everything.

We need more than ever to act on the pure, perfect, powerful love of our Father now and in the Next Place. All of us need to rest in the secure love of the Father. Allow the Holy Spirit and Jesus to show us the Father in our intimacy with God trough prayer.

God desires to lead us to places we cannot get to without the power of the Holy Spirit. If something has died in you or your life, God is moved by compassion. We have heard that people will never understand or connect to God. In the worst of times and the best of times, people are ignorant of the fires of love and the awesome power in drawing us to himself. God shows love for us and draws us into an intimate relationship. Our relationship with God is initiated by God. Our loving Father longs for us. When we attempt to connect, we do not know how, where, why, and when to begin. Believing that God is communicating with me through all of life, and that God knows me better than I know myself. In human relationships we reveal everything to cause any relationship to be fulfilling, honest, and more life changing. That is much more real as God in fullness welcomes us in sacred loving embraces. "The Lord sees the good people and listens to their prayer." (I Peter 3:12) We learn to pray by praying. Prayer is more caught than taught. When we commune with God, we present our fears, our dreams and desires, our needs, our questions, and we express our gratitude, joys, and offers of praise. The effects of God's love include a sense of hope, guidance, healing, meaning and purpose for our life's journey. We also join with God to participate in divine dreams for ourselves, friends and family, and the world. Praying also has an effect as we interact with God. When we behold the awesomeness of this relationship and fully realize what God has to offer each of us, we will pray like Paul. See Ephesians 3:14-21. Knowing that we are daughters and sons of God makes all the difference in living in the kingdom of God on earth. Prayer illuminates the love and the joy of knowing God is my Father. We can then have a foundation for loving other people and serving them with all our God-given gifts.

Paul Tournier, noted Christian physician and author from Geneva, Switzerland, enjoyed a spiritual life. He wrote many books in retirement. Tournier wrote in *The Healing of Persons* that the Bible, the Word of God, "shows Jesus going away by himself in the early morning to meet God face to face and receive orders for the day's work." (Tournier, Paul. *The Healing of Persons,* p. 286) He said that the doctor helps patients see the will of God. He noted the need for doctors who know how to pray and obey God. If he were an active physician, he would be in the middle of today's fight against today's virus. He cites three paths in front of every human being: reality without God and the dissociation of the materialists; God without reality, the dissociation of the pseudo-mystics; and God with reality, the difficult calling of Christian faith. (Tournier, Paul, *ibid.*, pp. 277-278)

Prayer is the doorway to heaven on earth. I enjoy reading books on techniques of prayer. Personal techniques help you connect in prayer, retreating to a quiet place without responsibility or distraction so that you anchor the sense of presence in your body, here, now, in this moment, in this secret place. The mystery and miracle are that we can call on the entire host of heaven to pray with us. After all, we are all praying together for ourselves and for the healing of the world.

The joy of intimacy is that it actually lives in your own soul, where sorrows are God's sorrows, and your dreams are in juxtaposition with God's dreams. Feel yourself surrendering to the loving arms of your protector. We can speak with a familiar and comfortable intimacy. This healthy image is of one who sees us and loves us as we are, one who feels strong and safe. Take refuge in this image that allows us to settle into the comfort of unconditional love. As I enjoy God, I pray this prayer: "I believe that the desire to please you does in fact please you. And I hope that I have the desire in all that I'm doing. I hope that I will never do anything apart from that desire. And I know if I do this, you will lead me by the right road, though I may know nothing about it. Therefore, I will trust you always though I may seem lost and in the shadow of death. I will not fear, for you are ever with me, and you will never leave me to face my perils alone."

Enjoying God is so beautiful and precious, a delight for you. It is being thankfully awake every day we live. "The kingdom is within you," Jesus said. The joy of God is unspeakable and infinite, as unfathomable as the countless blessings given to us now. Prayer is the spark that sets worship aflame.

As I wrote *Joy Comes in the Mourning: Love Is Forever*, I did rejoice in the confidence in the resurrection and that death is defeated. I know our tears will be wiped away. All the love I had for my brother David and God did not take away the futility, my depression and anger, my loss and the world's loss. My last words to the living David were, "David, I love you. Forgive me for anything I ever did or said that gave you harm."

Prayer is an exquisite opportunity to be grateful that you find joy in God. Allow your mind to become still. Take a few moments to recall the gifts and blessings you might have overlooked or took for granted. Let them ooze into your mind as you savor your life, your loved ones, your food and shelter, your delights, and nourishments that you enjoy. Offer your own blessing to each and every gift to your friends who accompanied you, those who cared for you, and to all that you were able to meet their needs. Julian of Norwich said, "Prayer fastens the soul to God." Prayer is the deep joy of intimate companionship that arrives step by step until we know the oneness of love.

Graced moments sweep us away with the joy of communion with love. Joy is divinity dancing inside of us. Joy is not something as new as we sometimes thank. In my research, I found an enlightening little story told by Saint Francis of Assisi. He tells of a cold winter when he arrived home to his monastery. He is not invited into the place and faced rejection. Francis related that God gave him patience and he was calm, not upset, and not suffering from rejection. His understanding of joy is deep as he finds himself with nothing, but nothing to lose. He found himself enjoying his conformity to the joy of salvation. Read Psalm 63. Joy is experienced when God is fully found without our expectations so that we store the videos and get an invitation to dance. True joy is not a fleeting thing.

Every moment in our life journeys is a gift, a sign of the kingdom come in us. We are now aware of the joys of prayer placing our soul's attention on every blessing we receive, each precious jewel that unveils the living presence of the kingdom of God with us today and forever.

Enjoying God and the joy of salvation has been the pathway from annihilation, from sin and stupidity, from possessiveness, and from unhappiness. When we reach out to others with unconditional love, we are being saved. When we find ourselves in the depths of our being intimate with God, we are saved. We enjoy God in a saving presence. Whatever brings surprises of joy be it making friends, dancing, writing, singing, preaching, making love, eating a good meal, running, walking, swimming, using artistic gifts is the joy of salvation, the joy of being saved. In our confidence, we pray, "May I experience the joy of life in your presence." Some theologies insist we avoid anything that leads to enjoyment or it is not an aspect of salvation. Puritanical groupies insist if it's hard, it has to do with salvation. Some insist that if it's done in church, it has to do with salvation, but if it's done at work or at home, it probably has nothing to do with salvation. Some believe salvation comes only after we die. We get a blissful life on after we leave this earth. It happens in heaven. Realizing that God is a saving presence now is a flashing joy for us. Some who do not believe this. They point to the deadly virus pandemic of our time, evil rulers of this world, hurricanes and tornadoes, bombs, earthquakes and accidents, injustices, exploiting the poor. Evil is a huge mystery. Sharing with God concerning our shadow is hard as we risk allowing our whole self to be revealed.

Human freedom is beyond understanding. God is love, and that love does not punish. Our sinful evil ways bring hurt to us, but it is not a punishment from God.

God is love. Love means we banish the notion that God deals with us in any hurtful way. Justifications for not praying fall away when we know the priceless value of enjoying union with God. We want to be united with the incredible mystery. As the years go by, I feel that I have fallen in love with God. And this is not just a one-way encounter. She/He/Spirit loves me too. It is always a quiet joy. These inner feelings involve a quiet and continuing persistence, and not unrestrained passion. When I have baptized new converts, they too respond that they have fallen in love with God.

We speak of a couple as "being in love." When someone is "madly in love" means ardent affection to a deep and unselfish concern, sensual satisfaction, and commitment to one another. Some express the thought of "being out of love." People fall in and out of love. When we write about intimacy and involvement with God, there is no possibility of our falling out of love. Love is the condition of our existence. To be a creature of God is to be always in love. To pray is to be aware that one is always in love. The presence of God is a saving presence. The joy of prayer enables me to be aware of the joy times I had in life, the great and small ones. The most radical joy came from the truth that I had been blessed with the grace of being born. The means the presence is a saving one not just a static one. God continues to give us life as the joy of salvation. God's salvation is more than just saving us from annihilation, but from our stupidity, our sin, our possessiveness. God is ever there with us waiting, encouraging, and calling. When we reach out to others with unconditional love, we are being saved. When we destroy those walls and build bridges of relationships, we are being saved. When we seek to know and accept ourselves in the depths of our being, we are being saved. When we replace a mere collective being together, we are being saved. In whatever way we may change our world view, our image of God in a unique experience of being saved.   We then know the *joy* of being saved. Joy is the link between heaven and earth, for in both places, there is rejoicing over the repentance of each sinner. Read Luke 15:7, 10. When the disciples were left alone after Jesus ascended to heaven, "they returned to Jerusalem with great joy." (Luke 24:52) Joy was the rationale of his calling. And the author of I John 1:4 said his purpose in writing was so "your joy may be full." Pray with assurance that "your sorrow will turn into joy" and "no one will take your joy from you" for Jesus came that "your joy may be full." (John 16: 20, 22, 24)

Prayer is the beginning and the end, the source, and the fruit the core and the content, the basis, and the goal of peacemaking.

~Henri Nouwen

Chapter Two

Sharing God's Dream

As I write today, the world is in the midst of a deadly endemic virus. In prayer, we reveal more and more who we are, and we come to realize who God is. We share with God and each other our hopes and dreams. We encounter God in a mysterious way. God wants a personal relationship with each one. If you were alive in the late summer of 1963, you probably heard Martin Luther King preach a sermon before 120,000 people and a media of millions from the Washington Monument. Tears may still be in your eyes as you think of hearing his sermon, "I Have a Dream." In my calling as the Minister of Joy to the World, I have often quoted King's anointed words throughout my world travels. The message is as pertinent today than any time in history. "I have a dream that one day this nation will rise up and live out the true meaning of its creed: 'We hold these truths to be self-evident, that all men are created equal. "I have a dream that one day on the red hills of Georgia the sons of former Slaves and the sons of former slave-holders will be able to sit down together at the table of brotherhood.

"I have a dream that my four children will one day live in a nation where they will not be judged by the color of their skin but by the content of their character."

God has been sharing God's dream in this world's complexity, in all the eons of evolution, millions of years of human activity in which each is allowed to act freely, even contrary to God's intentions. All the events that have ever occurred in the history of the universe, including the free action of every human. Prayer helps us come in tune, so that human happiness, in this world now and forever, as humans harmonize with God's dreams and intensions.

God has revealed these intentions in the writings of Holy Scripture. As the words of Martin Luther King's dream continues to influence my prayers and my life, with the words of Isaiah 2:3-5, 11:6-9. Read them now. As you read, think of the Next Place, a place of love and joy where there will be no more wars. Humans will no longer fear one another.

The path of prayer will help us to walk anywhere. There will be no tears, no diseases, no negative emotions. The dread of nuclear destruction and death will no longer linger like a pall over this world.

King's message ended with reading Isaiah 40:4-5. Handel used this scripture in the *Messiah*. This music has brought hope for generations. God's dream includes a place where all human beings can live as sisters and brothers in a community of joy united in the Holy Spirit with Jesus Christ, our brother, as sons and daughters of the Father, and in loving harmony with all there is. Paul sums this hope in Ephesians 1:3, 9-10. Meditate on his words now.

There can be no joy for anybody until there is joy finally for everyone. Prayer stirs us to love and act like God does. Our deepest dream is to live without fear and in eternal friendship with each other, we cannot discover God's intentions. Jesus told us that it is difficult to enter the kingdom of heaven. (Mark 10:26) Prayer is so essential, as Jesus also said, "With man this is impossible, but not with God; all things are possible with God." "I have a dream," God continues to tell us that our joy and our happiness is possible. Intimate prayer will fire us to keep stirring inside of us to desire with God the fulfillment even in the worst days on earth today. Read First John 4:7-21. "God is love" is the joy that we can assume. To understand that love is the nature of God alerts to an incredible freedom, a sense of lightness and joy. Can we possibly love as God loves?

Will we ever grow in the image of God in the way we love, forgive, and live our lives. We have not been "made perfect in love."

Jesus became an imitator of God through prayer. We must follow his example. We can get to know God by trusting in God's desires. And the dreams and desires inside of us as there is a reciprocal desire for intimacy with us as individuals as well as with us as a community. Prayer gives God an opportunity to reveal divine heart to us, and to open our hearts to God. Gradually, like Jesus, we become more like God in how we love, what attitude we hold, and when we feel the need for grace. In Jesus we find the mind and heart of God. Jesus wants to reveal himself. We need to keep alive the fire of desire for God and to know Jesus intimately. God will help us do the rest.

In the gospel of Thomas, a book of scripture that did not get into the canon of the church, reports Jesus as saying, "The one who is near me is near the Fire." That fire is God's love that purifies us. Once we are cleansed of sin, the fire consumes us as it were indistinguishable from the Fire. We find our own identity in the fire. And in prayer we come to know the Fire itself. As we pray, we first look inside ourselves. Looking outside ourselves, we will not bond with God. Within ourselves is the place where we discover God. I can sure understand the life and ministry of Vincent van Gogh. He had felt a call into ministry, and he received a theological education. Van Gogh's temper, his zeal and eccentric ways distanced him from the cultural traditions of the church. He was given a small parish in a poor coal-mining village. His preaching goal was to infuse a little light, a little hope, a little encouragement into their darkened lives. He was always deemed a little strange. Never appreciated by the church's powerful conservative leaders, history records that he lived among them, visited the sick, breathed the same coal dust into his lungs facing the danger of poisoned air as he prayed with them. He possessed a great fire in his soul. Few came to warm himself by his fire. He wanted to share his passionate fire, but people kept their distance and his response was deep depression. With years and years of rejection, loneliness, and deep unhappiness, his mental health deteriorated. He shot himself in the head while ending his life in a psychiatric institution for the insane. Vincent had been given two rooms where he could paint his meaningful art before he chose to die. A film was made of his life. It was titled *Lust for Life*.

In my freshman English class, my teacher Agnes Hull assigned me to write an essay on Tennyson's poem *Idylls of the King*. The theme records the dawn of English civilization during the reign of King Arthur. "More things are wrought by prayer than this world dreams of" is the thesis of the poem.

We become part of God's dream by choice. No one but God is essential to existence. When we "fall in love," we might say, "I cannot live without you." Of course, the lover can exist without that beloved one. The only one we cannot live without or exist with is God. Being separate from God, we simply are not. We do not exist. We are nothing. In the classic movie, it's a wonderful life, James Stewart's character is made aware of what live would be like if he never existed. Stewart was given a dream video of life in Pottersville because he never lived. During my dark days of the soul, I read the ancient book of Job. Read Job 33:14- 16. God speaks through words at times, but words are not the best way to communicate. As a writer, I am so aware of that truth. I cannot describe the fragrance of a rose in words. English words are difficult to translate into one's heart and soul. The expression, "a picture is worth a thousand words," reminds me as I view thousands of photos arranged like a scheduling personality does to keep the memories. Every Christmas, birthday, travels, my work as the Minister of Joy to the World. We attempt to express our intimate love for God through words. Sometimes cleaning the house, sending roses. Communication that has been halted because of the world pandemic such as holding a hand or rubbing a neck or shoulder. We can give gifts that are timely and personal showing the intimacy of the relationship.

Dreams have been a source for deepening faith. In the Bible we read the stories of Joseph and the pharaoh, those of Daniel and Nebuchadnezzer, about Joseph and the angel from God, of Joseph desire to flee into Egypt, about Pilate's wife, of visions throughout the Word of God. When we sleep, parts of a dream give clues concerning ourselves. Dreams are shared in support groups and with spiritual directors. The other side of consciousness is reflected in dreams. Dreams enrich and expand our intimacy in prayer.

To be in the presence of God is not a problem we deal with, for it is already and always there. It is the condition of being a created person. Awareness of God is not an action that we can do, but something we always are. Our attentive awareness brings us to discover what is God's dream. That closes the gap between us and God. Together and united we are part of the ultimate and loving dream of God. Knowing God's dream may not come in our quietude of praying but comes in the interaction with other people. It comes as we enjoy nature's beauty. This dream acceptance and awareness may come outside the hours we spend in prayer. However, the dream of God comes into our own dreams because of prayer. God spoke to Joseph in a dream with pictures sent into Joseph's mind. God even sent a dream to the cupbearer of the king. God used the image of grapes. Speaking to the king's baker, God used bread. Some dreams are dark and scary. A dream can be bright and full of sparkle. Another dream brings tears. Dreams are intimate communications whispered into our souls in the middle of the night. The fears and desires of our subconscious some pleasant, some frightening. I love to play basketball. One of my dreams was shooting basket after basket in a game. Some brought pleasure such as having a woman make love to me in a perfect way. Some brought awareness of somebody wanting to kill me. One night I dreamed that I was leading worship in a crowded church, but nobody paid any attention to me. I had an unbelievably effective sermon to deliver but no one wanted to listen to it. People then just got up and left the sanctuary.

Intimacy with God in prayer enables us to listen to what gives our heart sheer moments of joy. God guides us to find the passions of our souls. Dreams of doing something special that is in tune with our personalities and the dreams of childhood and youth as we hold and treasure God's calling for our lives.

We pray with serenity because we know that God is wise and loving. Wisdom joins our dreams with God whose desire for us is to recover from deaths, losses, and trials, and to triumph over tragedies. The will of God is bound up in the goodness of God. "Wisdom" uses even the negative experiences for raw materials to create good results.

 When we pray, "Thy will be done," we are surrendering our troubles over to God, expecting that good will to emerge as we benefit from God's power. Most people who find intimacy with God in prayer will not say that they are in love with God. I believe that God will never leave me and will support our mutual dream in good times or tough times. Keep saying, "Thy will be done." God is able to accomplish far more than all we ask or imagine. Grace is the loving movement of God's energy. We can never control grace. And we cannot rush to hurry the process. We obey and God does the rest.

God's dreams to us are in our language and in images known to us. The images are so personal, no one else could fully understand them. This is how much God intimately knows us. And loves us. The Father conveys how proud God is of us. As a father, I want to tell my family that. I used to tell my daughter stories about my own life, and I read to her books that enabled her to perceive the world. Often, I brushed my hand across her face, kissed her on the cheek, and told her how much I loved her. Bedtime was an opportunity for me to be with her in a special way. Her books were put back on the shelves, toys were put away, and in that stillness felt the power when we told each other we loved each other. I shall never forget the deep look she gazed into my eyes and quietly and lovingly just said, "Daddy."

Mental prayer in my opinion is nothing else than an intimate between friends; it means taking time frequently to be alone with Him, who we know loves us. The important thing is not to think too much and so do that which best stirs you to love. Love is not great delight, but desire to please God in everything.

~Saint Teresa of Avila

Chapter Three

The Joy of Answered Prayer

Answered prayer has brought splashes of surprising joy to many people. The joy of salvation connects us to the one who told his disciples that they could ask for anything from the Father and find that they are granted. Read and meditate on John 16:23-24; John 15:7-8, 11; I John 5:14-15. Look now at the context of these words of Jesus to understand him.

Jesus tells us to abide in him as intimately as branches abide in the vine. He repeats his promise to answer prayer as we abide in him. What a beautiful image is the vine and the branches. God's words must abide in us with the Spirit inside of us as we glorify God by the love in our lives to be joined as God's daughters and sons. The promises of Jesus assume this union.

We connect with God "in the name of Jesus." Dr. Jim Gordon preached a sermon on this at Elmwood Christian Church. My old friend and former regional minister in Nebraska, told us we must ask in accordance with God's intention and purpose, asking out of familiarity, as a name in the Bible means an invocation of Jesus' whole being, not just a way to get attention in our prayers.

Read I John 5:14-15 again. Before asking for something, we must consider before God whether the requests are made in the will, purpose, and dreams of God. When we have inner assurance with the will of God, we are given the divine confidence. I know from God's Word that the joy of salvation is offered to all, and that we pray with assurance that that is God's will.

Read James 4:2-4, 7-10. We need to come to God with a purity of heart. Many prayers are ineffective. James indicates the reasons. Read Isaiah 58:1-11. To make it short, sin can hinder prayer.

When your personal life does not seem to be bringing you joy, ask God to help you understand why. We all have experienced unexplained mysteries in our prayer lives. We must continue to pray and deepen our love of God.

Joyful and happy times when we feel peace and contentment affects our relationship with God. The goal is not to pray correctly to get answers. Read Romans 8:26-27.

We should never be surprised when God answers prayer. We may think we have finally learned to pray with the joy of answered prayer. Still we live many days feeling God is not listening. Even Jesus' disciples said, "Teach us to pray." They wanted to know not only how to pray but also what to pray for. Read the Sermon on the Mount, especially Matthew 6:1-13. Here Jesus gives insight into the spiritual conditions and the specific kind of pray that God always answers. This sermon adds flesh to way that we pray. And it gives ways not to pray. Praying like a hypocrite includes the wrong motive. The hypocrite prays to impress other people. We tend to rush into prayer without preparation. God does not care for long lengthy prayers or loud prayers. Meaningless repetition is the root of our using too many words.

The Joy of Answered Prayer Comes with Sincerity

Jesus does not condemn public prayers, but he does not like pray to be "seen by men." Impure, selfish words with unworthy motives invades the most sacred place wiping dirty feet on the carpet of God's throne room. Prayer is not a spiritual status system. So many ministers pray eloquent prayers. People praise the beauty of these prayers. Often, they are delivered with a kind of ministerial tone. Prayers were a part of his performance calling attention to self rather than God to gain applause rather than the joy of the blessing of sincere prayers. Some constantly call attention to the many hours spent in prayer. In my home church, we had many all-night prayer meetings. It became difficult to keep awake. We prayed about numerous things and we were honest and sincere. Our intensions were pure. We did not pray in a secret place and afterward, most told everybody about this experience.

Jesus never meant that we were not ever to pray in public. If we do public praying, we should keep the connection going by private prayer. "Pray to the Father" is the secret Jesus shares. We have all attended prayer meetings where each person prays aloud. The prayer elicits "amens" with every phrase. When it is my turn, I am tempted to say something that will be appreciated with some "amens."

The experience may also include preaching to the gathered group. One man in one of my churches used the communion prayers to say what he wanted us to hear. In sincere prayer, the focus is on the Father concentrating on God's presence, the divine will and glory. Effective prayer meetings cause us to be conscious of God than the presence of others. To shut out the world, we shut ourselves out with God. Ineffective prayer meetings are meetings where people said prayers as if there was no one in the place but them and God. Nothing will give satisfaction to the hypocrite but the praise of other people. Nothing brings satisfaction for those who pray with God in sincere ways but the praise of God. Sincere prayer is not just about us, but about the family of God far and near. I have no right to ask for something that I would not want every member of the family of God to possess. Prayer is not a way that I can get ahead of others, occupy a more powerful position, or to help my local home congregation to attract a bigger audience with more wealth than any other church.

God remains free to act on the Lord's dreams and intentions. We all have errors in our image of God and in the anticipation in our mental image of God answering our prayer. If our theology, our cultural faith, tends to hold on to past images and that there is only one way for problems to be solved. I love to give red roses to those I appreciate and love. As a boy I thought all roses were red. Beautiful red roses were planted by my mother. One day I noticed a neighbor grew yellow roses. In later years in my travels, I saw a thousand colors in a park in Munich. That's much like God's revelation of possibilities and mysteries. When we go on to the Next Place, we will know that God always acted in the right way. Sometimes I think God waits until the situation is humanly impossible.

The Holy Spirit will show us that God's ways are not our ways. As a minister of joy, I have traveled the world telling people how to pray. In all my pastorates, I insisted on a prayer ministry. When our congregation would need direction, we would begin by 100 consecutive days of prayer in groups of three people. Now during this dangerous endemic corona virus, God has led me to write this book. God is bigger than our culture, our greed, or theology. Any person's concept of prayer will never limit or bind God. God is not limited by time to listen to our requests. Read Isaiah 65:24.

God unveils in divine wonders in ways we fail to be aware of. Most do not that "earth's crammed with heaven," as Elizabeth Barret Browning wrote. Or as Gerard Manley Hopkins wrote, "the world is charged by the grandeur of God." God's revelations come as a surprise as they may turn the world upside down. Some revelations disturb us and show our dark side, our greed, and our selfishness. Others reveal how much God loves us and that we are a great concern.

When we turn our minds and hearts to God, God invites us into a life- giving relationship that is new and unending. With God love is forever. God is the one from whom all life flows, the one who restores and heals our brokenness, the one who empowers us to share that love with others.

God answers prayer for God's glory. God answers according to the Divine dream. When we ask God to meet our needs, we are praying in the will of God. Jesus prayed, "Father, glorify your name." That is what we can say when we do not have the words. Whatever we pray for, it is certain that the glory of God takes precedence. God always has the best thing in mind, never compromising the plans that God has in the ultimate dream for us. We can then pray as Jesus prayed in Luke 22:42, Father, if it is your will, remove this cup from me; nevertheless, not my will, but your will be done."

God reveals love through Jesus. We must give up our preconceived and erroneous ideas of God. Thinking of God as a harsh judge or someone far away hinders us from knowing and accepting what God wants to share with us. We do not rule the world, nor do we own it. Prayer restores humankind into God's image. When we observe a daughter and her mother or a son to his father, we use the term "spitting image." Were it not for our differing ages and our gray hair, wrinkles, and Physical weaknesses, it could be difficult to tell a parent from a child? Like our Father, we are called to be filled with the joy of our salvation. We are to be kind, patient, compassionate, and loving. The image of God has been tarnished, almost obliterated. We need a refurbished transformation so we can find our true self and our truth, beauty, and goodness. God's beauty washes over our souls, cleansing us of ugly dispositions and mean-spirits. Prayer brings us into the presence of Jesus. Without the prayer connection, we soon lose our identity, our dignity, our imaging of God. We become illiterate in our understanding and become blind to the gospel of love and forgiveness. Prayer is the pathway where the memory of Jesus is kept alive and keeps its power to shape us. The Word of God went forth, became flesh, and dwelt among us. Every word and deed of Jesus' life became the means and the message through which God redeemed the world. God continues to speak through Jesus and the language of our own lives.

Remember the song, "Love is a many splendored things." Love brings energy into the world that we can receive and give away to people who are starved for love. Augustine described God's grace in writing, "Because You have loved me, O Lord, you have made me lovable." In prayer we can experience splashes of love. if we abide in the Light, we are blessed and cleansed.

Prayer really is hard work. God takes the first step toward us. Prayer is God's gift. We are graced to share in God's life, so we are enabled to pray. This yoke becomes easy and the gift is a source of joy. Perhaps having to work at prayer serves to make it more valuable and significant. We keep working at it every day of our lives. Prayer struggles cause us to lean on God. Calling on God with prayer and believing that God listens to words is to exercise faith.

Elizabeth Barrett Browning wrote, "God answers sharp and sudden on some prayers, and thrusts the thing we have prayed for in our face, a gauntlet with a gift in it." Prayer is the doorway to blessed assurance. Harry Emerson Fosdick has a chapter on unanswered prayer. He quotes Habakkuk 1:1-4, then writes, "Complaint about unanswered prayer is nothing new. Consider this cry of distress with which Habakkuk opens his book. Read Habakkuk 1:1-4. "Let us consider the unreasonableness of allowing such experiences to cause the abandoning of prayer." (Fosdick, Harry Emerson, *The Meaning of Prayer*. New York: International Committee of Young Men's Christian Association, 1915, p. 113. Fosdick wrote that we are unfitted to substitute our wish for God's will. In the old out of print volume, that appalling results would follow if all our requests were answered. We fail to remember how often God answers our prayers. He always says that perhaps God is suggesting ways we can answer our own requests. We might not be giving God enough time. Even when God does not choose to answer prayer affirmatively, he does answer. Paul's petition from his physical distress was not answered in the affirmative, but Paul was answered. Paul wrote the answer in II Corinthians 12:9, "My grace is sufficient for thee; for my power is made perfect in weakness." The father of existentialism, Soren Kierkegaard, overwhelms us with his 800-page work, The Prayers of Kierkegaard, dazzles us with sayings such as "Teach me Lord not to make a martyr of myself through stifling reflection. Teach me to breathe deeply in faith." He desired to know himself before knowing anything else, including God. In his unhappy childhood, his father took the children to the cemetery where he told them to dwell on the agony of Jesus as they were to confess their sins.

As he grew into adulthood, Kierkegaard repelled by his father's conservative Lutheran faith. He studied theology at the University of Copenhagen, where his faith in the weighty old orthodox Christian dogma shifted and cracked. He stopped praying to the avenging distant deity God. No divine being would have nothing to do with Soren's little life and his encompassing quest for meaning. He tried all else before considering the radical, cure of Jesus. It was not a medicine he wanted to take.

On May 19, 1838, Soren had a decisive spiritual conversion, a feeling of indescribable joy, that was inexplicable to his rational mind. Like in John Wesley's conversion, he felt "his heart strangely moved." He embraced his joy of salvation as a passion, a leap to live life in its fullest sense. His spiritual life rejected the ways of the Evangelical Lutheran Church of Denmark. His writing reflected his statement, "The function of prayer is not to influence God, but rather to change the nature of the one who prays."

Soren abandoned his calculated safety for a reckless and passionate life with Jesus. He attributed his frequent prayer for his inward transformation as intimate prayer became as valuable to him as breathing. Praying became his source of the highest happiness, the joy of salvation. Soren frankly writes his questions to God, his pain, consolation, suffering, doubts, love, longing, and depression. He was full of thanks to God.

Prayer does not change God, but it changes him who prays.

~Soren Kierkegaard

Chapter Four

Going on in Intimacy with God

The path to intimacy with God is not an easy road. As I write, I am experiencing so much pain, deep grief, and volumes of advice during the pandemic. Millions have died and we have lived this horror together.

We must make prayer a regular habit. Building a rewarding and faithful prayer life requires persistent prayer. Prayer must be an on-going focus. Perseverance counts. Believing that God will answer today, tomorrow, or next year on my schedule, is not praying without ceasing. God wants our persistence. The discipline of sustained prayer brings us joy. God is not one of convenience, but God has a timing, so keep praying in the Spirit with endurance. Live in faith. Experiences with prayer come with both satisfaction and struggle. In going on with God, a regular pattern of prayer is needed, a pathway that works for you. Keep practicing the approaches to prayer not only by yourself, but with your brothers and sisters. Praying "without ceasing" is a challenge. Take time for regular acts of praying several times each day. Perhaps in the beginning, you could just say, "thank you" about ten times a day. There is spiritual danger when prayer becomes an afterthought that happens only occasionally in unpredictable ways. Effective prayer is a "life pattern" or a human habit. If we refuse to pray, we feel its absence. Think of prayer as a vital habit, a rhythm that keeps life going on. It is a special date with God. As our eternal lover, God lures us back into this presence with delight and expectation. We are glad as human lovers enjoying each moment

Faithful praying is a habit. In our habit, we can now approach prayer with more intention, more attention, and more reflection. We feel more spiritually fit, energized, and passionate about connecting to God. As your praying bears spiritual fruit, feel free to increase the frequency. We have more times on some days than other times, perhaps in the evening hours than in the morning. Use your time as best as you are enabled. Our spiritual intention is to pray regularly, not to log a specific amount of time.

Some find comfort and nourishment when they pray as they look at a Bible, a cross, or a piece of art that keeps focus on Jesus and the story of our redemption. You may pray sitting in a chair, kneeling, or standing.

Christians and non-Christians have never been strangers to sickness and illness. Church history has recorded numerous deadly events. Between the years 249-262, a deadly pandemic swept through the city of Rome and more than 5,000 people each day during its peak. Just as the first responders, nurses, doctors, truck drivers, and thousands of people on the front lines, believers in Jesus cared for the sick, even at risk of their own health. The Roman rulers offered no real help. Self-preservation kicked in for the majority, but as in our day, a minority rose up in love and compassion. People noticed.

I would be less than honest if I were not to tell you of the experience of darkness that always comes in intimacy with God. This reality is not an awareness of failure or regression. In a mysterious way, the connection gets better in times of uncertainty and drought.

Faith brings a deep conviction that God desires to dwell with us and in us in loving covenant. The joy in prayer comes as we attune ourselves to God's presence. We become confident of God's help as we go on with God, relying on that love, not ourselves, and so we progress toward God's dream. God continues to offer amazing grace to we who were lost and blind. The joy of salvation brings the promise that your life will take on a quality and depth of living you could never imagine.

The soul living in darkness is far from despair. The darkest moments are just before the dawn. When this divine dawn suddenly breaks, and the whole long night that has passed will be a small price to pay for the healing joy of the new day.

God breaks into our lives, and life is lived in color not black and white. God is ingenious, all-knowing. Love comes in the relationship we have with a sister or brother, or even in the pain of a broken relationship. God may speak in nature, in the taste of food, the song of a bird, and experiences that offer an opportunity of grace. Prayer is the encounter of our thirst with the thirst of God. Prayer is an on- going love relationship. Prayer is a dialogue between two people who love each other. Prayer is much more than words. It is the natural expression of love toward God. Read I Thessalonians 5:17.

Going on with God in prayer is not a luxury. The connectional gift is more than a friendly invitation. Prayer is a command, a necessity. God will give us all the resources we need. We are temples of the Holy Spirit who prays within us. The Spirit gives us a new heart so that we may hear and do God's word. Going on with God reveals that we are in those who do God's will. Others continue to hold on to their wills. We ponder, hear whispers, feel nudges that come from God. In our secret private place, we enter into silence and solitude seeking the thoughts of the Holy Spirit. God often whispers something and at first you might not even hear it. Trust God in your comings and goings. It will turn out right.

Even if one sees the dark times as a purification, one wants to see it end. We might come to accept that a healing surgery is necessary, we would not want to spend the rest of life on an operating table. Permanent and perpetual surgery does not lead to renewed health and fruitful living. If we came to realize that would be our continuous fate, we would let death come and not prolong the agony. Living in the intimacy of God is the beginning of eternal life. Prayer is the foundation of an eternity of loving God. Even after we spent a million years in heaven, we will continue to know and love God. If this work lasts every year of our lives on earth, those years will be short lasting from the perspective of eternity of loving and being loved by God.

In my book, *Joy Comes in the Mourning: Love Is Forever*, I share my eternal love for my brother David. When I received copies of my book with UPS, I looked up and said, "David, you will enjoy my tribute to you." I pray connected to David as he lives in heaven. Millions of Christians continue to connect with those who have died. And they are praying for us. That's the meaning of the phrase "communion with the saints." The Bible shares little about this type of praying.

In First Corinthians 15:29, Paul mentions "baptism for the dead." I heard an Easter service prayer from the Shine of the Immaculate Conception that reflected on baptism for those living and dying in Christ. It still gives me comfort as I pray for David and others that I have known. And it is a joy as they pray for me. Most of the enshrined saints are departed from the earth. As we become older, we get nearer to our time of completing our life journey. C.S. Lewis said, "At our age the majority of those we love best are dead. What sort of intercourse with God could I have if what I love best were unmentionable to God?"

I have known a pervasive inner joy that comes from constant fellowship with God. I pray the joy of the Lord has bubbled out to the world. Prayer is the first thing on my lips in the morning and the last activity before I sleep. I want to be known as a man who walked and talked with Jesus. On my tombstone, I pray they chisel the words, "Minister of Joy to the World."

My brother Edward W. McReynolds always looked up to Dr. Albert Schweitzer. During medical school, my brother had a framed picture with the inspiring words of this remarkable man. Schweitzer often dreamed in his childhood. He and his family went on holiday to Colmar, France. The child was moved by a statue of an African man in chains. His lovely shaped body rippled with strength. The slave's eyes revealed a melancholy stare. Schweitzer could not forget this expression of thoughtful sadness. He was man of intimate connection to God through prayer. He prayed about the suffering in the world. He spent many of his youthful and young adult years in study and preparation. He earned doctor's degrees in religion, music, and philosophy.

Schweitzer read a report from the Paris Missionary Society in 1904. He felt a call to serve in Africa. He decided it more valuable to go as a physician and not a commissioned missionary. It took him nine more years to obtain his Doctor of Medicine degree. He built a small hospital in the jungle in what was then French Equatorial Africa, where he treated thousands of people and inspired millions including my brother Edward. My brother served as a pediatrician in Delaware for more than 50 years, the same number of years that Schweitzer served in Africa. My brother gave his life unselfishly in his calling from God. One memory of Ed in his childhood was his interest in being a physician. He would build model skeletons of the human body. He enjoyed playing with a little girl named Angie who had dreamed of becoming a nurse and enjoyed those precious times of playing together.

As a young boy I prayed for my brother Ed. We enjoyed God and our lives. Sometimes we fought, disagreed, or lived in competition with each other. One year we attended a Vacation Bible School at Woodlawn Baptist Church in Bristol, Tennessee. The pastor offered to give a Thompson's Chain Reference Bible to the student who presented the best results in learning about the Bible. I believed God had called me to become an ordained minister. While Ed read many medical books from the Bristol Public Library, I read books on the Bible and the vocation of ministry. When the time came for the pastor to award the Bible, Ed's work was deemed better than mine. I was a bit embarrassed. Deep in our souls, we loved each other. We still feel proud of the joy that God has given to us on our earthly journey.

We find joy in the assurance that God is with us during every day of our time on earth. God walks with us. God talks with us. God is intimately involved in our lives. Intimate moments bring us insight that cannot be easily explained. Those moments come when God has touched our lives like the morning sun shining through our bedroom window. The moment offers something eternal. In those sun-drenched experiences filled with love and grace, we hear and enjoy who God is, and where God guides us. Enjoying God means listening to what makes our souls glad. Joy comes as we unearth the passions of our living that may have buried during our childhood and youth.

Through the intimacy of being with God, we find a love that sustains in evil, fear, or suffering. God's love holds us together despite our illnesses. In my book, *Dancing with Bipolar Bears*, I talk about peace and suffering. The more we love, the more we become aware the more we are set free. We are blessed even with illnesses with joy, hope, and meaning despite the obstacles. With ongoing assurance, we can with grace and grit know that nothing can harm me, nothing at all because I am loved by God. This spring morning, I am enjoying the sunrise from my breakfast room table. I'm drinking tea as I engage in intimate communion with the God of all creation. I can view the park, the Christian Church building, flowers, and stillness. Each new day, my journey begins anew. This ongoing intimacy causes me to be aware that time and space are not in our control.

We see leaves darken and fall, the ice, snow, fog, and frost come with the barrenness of winter. We mourn family and friends as they get sick and die. We now live with a virus pandemic that could end human existence on the earth. We increasingly wonder, can life itself be saved. It does not matter how long and firmly we grasp and hold on to love and life as our human relationships, hopes, dreams, possessions, and desires slip through our fingers. We are powerless in loving better and we regret what we experienced as we hold on to that beautiful day, the moment of love, and the hope for happiness. We feel desperate as day passes into night. Over and over, I plead Jesus have mercy on me. Jesus has opened a way to save us from death. Passing from death to the glory of life forever, Jesus has promised that if we hunger for the joy of salvation, we can enjoy a new relationship with Love. Life is now not subject to sin and death. We keep in communion with and eventually discover that the Father of Jesus is now our Father.

Science, the church, and the atmosphere of the world say that without a good earthly father, one can never understand to have God as a Father. Those who suffered abuse and neglect from their father can experience the love that God can give. I know personally of the power of God working in those whom I encounter and lead in psychotherapy and prayer. They can become souls bursting with the Love of their Father. The base for Jesus's desire for his disciples is that they come to know

God as their Father. In the last days of his earthly journey, he communicated urgently that these disciples know the intimacy with God as Father that Jesus had. Read John 14:8.

Let your mind be filled with Christ. Cling to him. It is a friendship. In the beginning of an intimate friendship, we do know much about the one we have friended. One takes hold of the thoughts of another. The influence continues to be made stronger. Every part of the souls is brought under the influence of imagination, affection, and memory. In intimate prayer, there is growing exchange and Jesus will be felt in our every activity. The soul becomes refreshed and the will invigorated as the eye stretches beyond the present and sees the accomplished ending.

Normal fluctuations come with our days of ongoing prayer. Our physical and psychological well-being inevitably affects our experience with God. Ask God to help you find the root of the cause of the laxity or unfaithfulness. Missing prayer times or cutting them short, or our tolerating new sin in our lives will cause you to know a dark period of dry runs. Prayer, just like a physical exercise, becomes difficult if we do it only sporadically. Just a few years ago, I got really fit. I could play basketball at the Lincoln Racquet Club with younger men. Finally, I hit 77 consecutive free throws in one session. Our experience of intimacy will deepen through the dark dry nights of the soul. During those times we are tempted to shorten our prayers or to just drop them off our schedule. The Bible warns us that none of us will be spared trials and does not magically spare us of trials and suffering. God has a permissive will. Read Romans 8:28. God can bring great good out of the events of our lives. God does not intend for us to accept but to resist and overcome. Thousands felt this during the epidemic that struck the world. Read James 4:7-8. Suffering can be borne joyfully. Now read I Peter 12-16. Reducing our prayer time in our secret places. We need the love and encouragement of others to take our prayer time. The men at Washington Chapel United Methodist Church in Abingdon, Virginia would meet and pray for me and our worship. They also gave me time in the mornings to spend in prayer. Prayer time can be too long or too short. If we piously take too long, it becomes another burden. If it's too short, it will not allow the Holy Spirit to guide us.

Lack of peace and joy is a clear signal that we need to take care of problems. Asking the Holy Spirit to remind us that there is nothing more important than being with God. Anything that appears urgent is really inconsequential in the eternal perspectives of God's dreams for us. God has already given us the courage we need. As your prayer connection goes on, use what God has gifted to you. Go. It is for all to embrace. The Creator did not give the gift of God only for just us. With the guiding light of the Holy Spirit, we understand that this love includes all and excludes none. The ones we might feel to leave out are the ones in greatest need of our speaking to God on their behalf. Those at the bottom layers of society, or perhaps the body of Christ, we are invited to reach out and help someone through the gift of the power of prayer.

God does not need us for accomplishing divine things with vision, power, and ultimate capacity. He chooses to involve us. When we go on to the Next Place, we will be delighted to find that everybody owes somebody something. We will meet, and those who prayed for us, and many of the ones we prayed for us. We will get a glimpse of the untold riches made available in intimate prayer. Our prayers for others are signs of our love for them and for the One who first loved us. Prayer is for all even the feeble voice utters it far from the crowd or the organized church. It's easy to pray for the hungry, the jobless, the troubled and the downtrodden without trying to better their place in life. Christian people who pray must tear down the barriers and expand the work of praying to the huge dimensions of the whole world.

My grandmother, Anna Brewer, played the piano for the Salvation Army Church in Bristol, Virginia. She was never trained, but she played beautifully on the piano. Her home had a dirt floor and chickens ran through the house. She suffered much in her small Spencer Street home.

She played by ear. Her favorite hymn was "Precious Lord, Take My Hand" written and composed by Thomas Dorsey in 1932 after the deaths of his only son and his wife. She enjoyed Dorsey's other gospel songs, such as "Stand by Me," "We will Meet Him in the Sweet by and By," and "There'll Be Peace." My parents would say, "Jimmy, don't forget where you came from," I thought of that church filled with poor and simple people, who despite crude Appalachian culture, God was fully present, and the joy of the Lord was their strength. I can hear them singing now.

Precious Lord, take my hand,
Lead me on, let me stand,
I am tired, I am weak, I am worn,
Through the storm, through the night
Lead me on to the light,
Take my hand, precious Lord,
Lead me home."

To gather with God's people in united adoration of the Father is as necessary to the Christian life as prayer.

~Martin Luther

Chapter Five

The Joy of Praying with Others

When we pray, we never pray alone. Prayer guides us inward. We are led into deep communion with everyone who has ever prayed. Being intimate with God, we pray for and with the entire family of creation. We are part of something bigger than ourselves. In complete solitude in our secret place, we are joined with a loving community. The joy of connecting to the fabric of life brings grace and the alleviation of suffering for every soul in the world.

Even during this deadly COVID19 virus endemic, we cannot live apart from the dance of interdependence. God works through farmers, truck drivers, doctors, teachers, carpenters, nurses, artists, and writers. When we pray for peace and healing, we look for the benefits for all who are in need. With millions dying from disease, we feel overwhelmed by those many needs. We feel discouraged that we could not show our love by doing what we can do. There is awesome power in private prayer. God hears and answers as we pray alone in our comfortable praying places. There is also that same awesome power is experienced as we pray in groups of other believers, even if with only one other person. Expect great things from God in your prayers of agreement. As we pray in the presence of others, we vibrate love, wisdom, and grace. Remember, Jesus said that we could do the same miracles that he did, and even greater ones. Read John 14:12.

We grow in our union with God with support from others. Only with considerable support from others, have I been able to go on with God. Read Ephesians 5:18-20. As our commitment grows, our commitment to one another grows. In enjoying God's love more, the intention is that we love one another more and more. Love gives us a new relationship with one another. Read Acts 2:43-47. Community is not an option as we persevere in prayer. God desires our togetherness, not only for our own sake, but for the sake of the world. Jesus is the model of total awareness of God. He not only had a full consciousness of God, but of all reality in God. He experienced the meaning of our oneness with one another.

Jesus' death was for us, not himself. It was not a transition into total awareness of the Father. He already had that total awareness. It is clear that the fullness of the divine existed in him. Read I Corinthians 12:12, 25. In Paul's theology the phrase "in Christ" indicates we are not persons in isolation, but in oneness with one another. One way we can describe the Spirit of Joy Church is that it is a communion of women and men who experience oneness with Christ. It is sad that some believe church is remote, impersonal, and outside themselves. Church is a love relationship quite capable of releasing sentiments of love and endearment, such as any couple in love.

When we pray alone, praying for others in the stillness, we are not lonely. We are aware of our family and friends, especially those recently departed, we taste the companionship with God. Every prayer shapes the world for children and those who take the mantle of life after we have gone. I think that is what attracts me to the word and work of evangelism. International evangelism depends on visible groups of Christians who demonstrate in their life together the reality of God's love and the identity of Jesus as the Savior of the world. We must die to only an individual life but to commit to share the joy with others. We are one part of one body. Making choices and deciding how to use energy is to live in subordination to the overall good. When I wrote of my search for a perfect church community. In my book *Spirit of Joy Church*, I was told of churches whose members are cold, indifferent, superficial, and all filled and directed by guilt, anger, fear, and anxiety. Few in these congregations have made a deep and personal commitment to the God that they are supposed to worship. The spirit of God is fired to bring renewal. Exempting ourselves from community is to exempt us from the flaming fire that is the love of God.

Love God and love your neighbor as you are loving yourself. Offer your gifts and graces to the whole family of God. Forgive those who hurt you. Seek first the kingdom of God, and all these treasures from God shall be given to us. God is your family home, and all will be well.

As a counselor and as a pastor, I have given my gifts to those addicted to drugs, sex, gambling, and such utter brokenness as they shared stories of sorrow and hope. The moment always comes when they must confront difficulties and problems too complex and enormous to deal with by themselves. With the heavy weight of extraordinary losses, challenges unmet, responsibilities unfulfilled, and rejections at every corner, we may be tempted to try to solve our problems by ourselves. The results are to become weary, depleted, exhausted, and totally overwhelmed. In prayer we offer what we cannot do ourselves, and place our burdens in larger, wiser, and more powerful hands.

Ignatius of Loyola said, "Act as if everything depended on you, and trust as if everything depended on God." Quietly reflect on these words as you are invited to take on a deeper trust in dependence and faith in God. Let these practical words breathe with your breath. As you do what you have the power to do, let go and let God.

The Holy Spirit brings us not only into a relationship of joy and love, but into a new relationship with one another. The Holy Spirit was given on the day of Pentecost and he brought a change in how the early Christians lived with each other. That way of life brought them into a community where they cared for each other, shared their lives together, and experienced themselves as sisters and brothers in the new family.

Pentecost brought the experience of God's love being poured into them through the spirit that freed them from the pride, fears, and resentments that kept them apart. God created the human race for community. Read Acts 2:43-47. Together and in all periods of time God has used community to do awesome things. Keep these truths in your mind that because of the immense love of God causes us to desire God and one another.

Praying for others means praying for our loved ones and the larger human community. Prying for others means praying with others at their request. The praying community involves a deep trust that the will of God and what is best for the situation or the person. The outcome might not be what we have chosen. In my earlier days, churches had Wednesday night prayer meetings. As a pastor, I still do. During my ten years of service with the First Christian Church in Weeping Water, Nebraska, we prayed through all 150 psalms using the Eugene Peterson translation.

I personally can testify that it has been through the support and encouragement of others that I have been able to go on with God. It is part of the dream of God that everyone in the family give support and love. Some doubt that they have the ability to persevere and respond. Every Christian can by support that comes from being part of a community with a spirit of joy. Common life together helps us to respond to the word of God in a variety of forms within the fabric of our daily life journeys.

As our commitment grows, God's intention is that our commitment to each other also grows. As we love God more and more, the intention is that we love one another more and more. Loving God and loving neighbor are exactly the same call. Read John 17:20-23. The loving union is not complete until we are one with another. We prefer to be in company with women and children who are obviously attractive to those with whom I share this bond with Christ. We are each a part of the body as we make decisions and live in subordination to the world's overall good. We sense that God will do something major and central to our lives. Out of God's immense love we enjoy being with our Father and with one another now and forever.

I often pray with a partner as I pray for others. I have some fellow ministers. to meet with in a regular time. During the pandemic I use the telephone or technology as we keep social distance rather than engaging in person. At times I light a candle reminding me of the promises of Jesus that he will be there even in the meeting of one or two or three. Some Christians go to someone for spiritual direction with one who is trained, experienced, and gifted in assisting people. With few words the director can enable you to see where God is at work, drawing you deeper into intimacy with God. A monk and brother of the Benedictine monastery in Conception, Missouri was such a rich resource in my spiritual development.

As a retired minister, I am asked to preach or to lead weekend Vision Quests for joy with hurting church communities. During one experience, the congregation had lost its pastor under circumstances agonizing and traumatic for that pastor and the church. As I shared the grief with remaining church members, our shared prayers, I realized that our gathering together was not only a hurting group of individuals. The people had a personality knitted in sorrow. Some wounds are passed on through decades. Some unhealed pain becomes the emotional atmosphere that sinks into the subconscious souls.

I think one thing is that prayer has become useful, interesting, fruitful, and almost Involuntary in my life.

~Mary Oliver

Chapter Six

Incomparable Benefits of Prayer

The Word of God tells us that God offers incomparable benefits to those living in intimate love. God invites us into an intimate relationship. In prayer, God stands with us throughout all the seasons of our lives. Read Psalm 103:1-2. We are never alone. One benefit is that become more like Jesus and to live as he did. We continue to be thankful for these gracious gifts.

When I was a younger man, I enjoyed running. Now I can only walk. I enjoy a stroll in nature's beauty. I pray as I view the birds, animals, birds, insects, trees, plants, the wind, and the sun. These walks have benefited me to learn things about myself, God, live, and my calling. Music benefits us when we are tired. Fresh air, flowers, touching a tree becomes an act of prayer.

 God the shepherd, God the vine, God the initiator longs to share life with us as part of our loving bond. God surrounds us with an immense power that is an indescribable benefit. God has no limits of love. God chooses to work through our consciousness. Perhaps this God's holy self-limitation. God waits for our consent. God is concerned with the awakening of human consciousness on every level. We are not lifeless channels as prayer benefits us. In God's divine ecology we enjoy the benefits of connection.

Prayer Changes Us

We will pass into another atmosphere where love reins. We focus on living not dying. We give all our strength and energy in the loving work of God. We go on upward into a life of joy.

We gain a new revelation of the setting the soul free to live a life of joy. These moments of joy come with the assurance of our acceptance and the love of God might come with overwhelming rushes of emotion.

From birth to death, we can become aware in the joy and beauty of prayer. Praying is not just to gain the significant benefits. We cannot overlook the delight that comes when we are invited and accept the joys of the presence of God. A faithful approach to prayer recognizes that God has charge over our lives. We pray in response to God and out of thankfulness for the benefits that Jesus tells us about during his brief ministry.

In the dark nights we sense that our prayers have gone unanswered or that we did not get what we desired or expected. Focusing on ourselves, our needs, and what we must do to get God to help us meet them makes us blind to what God is already doing that sustains and nourishes. A prayer life with benefits shows us we are not God. Our faithful prayer shows that God has charge over our lives. We are thankful for everything God has already done for us through Christ Jesus. God acts in grace as Jesus invited us to pray. The Holy Spirit has empowered us. Our prayer is a response to God being God.

The purpose of prayer is not to take the initiative in our relationship to God. We are not telling God what we need to convince God to provide for us. It's to our joy and benefit to offer a faithful response to the grace-filled initiative that God has already taken on our behalf with a promise to endure. Remember, God is in charge before we pray when we pray, and after we pray.

As a child of God, you have the benefit of instant intimacy. God's calendar is always cleared. You will face God's full attention. Proverbs 15:8 assures us, "He delights in the prayers of the upright." The more we come into the presence of God, the more natural and comfortable we will be around God. God desires our intimacy and fellowship. We are free to come boldly. Amazing! God loves to be with us. Psalm 145:18 informs us, "The Lord is close to all who call on (God,) to all who call with sincere love." The word we need to emphasize is "sincere."

God will be God. As God's sons and daughters, our prayer response is to mirror what Jesus has given us. Intimate prayer enables us to live closer to the example of Jesus. Jesus invites us to prayer precisely because of the benefits make an enormous difference. We are made aware of this as we pray, we think about what happens by how it brings benefits. (Psalm 103:2)

Just as Jesus demonstrated, prayers give many benefits. These benefits are essential in every aspect of life included the relational, emotional, physical, and beyond anything we could imagine.

In John 21:25, we are told of the unbelievable works that Jesus accomplished. "If every one of them were written down, I suppose that the world could not contain the books that would be written."

In prayer, solidarity with God and other people, intimacy with God, and joy in faithfulness are beneficial beyond number. On-going prayer requires time, attention, effort, interest, and commitment. Our prayer life cannot be sustained without intentional effort. Nothing draws us to God and God to us like prayer. Intimacy reveals images of familiarity, closeness, knowledge, and experience, deep understanding, and significant affection for each other. Our intimate relationship does not prevent the freedom of God apart from us.

Read Psalm 34:18, 145:8. God remains near and hears us when we speak. Holy Scripture conveys God's dream to be intimate and present, and to be a heavenly parent. This prompts us to clarify our relationship with God and deepen our responsibility to live as God desires.

Praying for the Whole World

When we pray there are benefits that reach all God's children. A Texas woman who attended one of my prayer conferences in Waco said, "Believing in the power of prayer has made all the difference in my life. I used to feel terribly sorry for myself the day I was diagnosed with multiple sclerosis. I felt my life was useless. My pastor told me to pray with my eyes on others and not just myself. I have more free time as I am confined to this wheelchair. I have learned that prayer give benefits for coping with anything." Incredible stories have been shared by young people, people living in nursing homes, in jails and prisons. What a joy when I experience faces that light up like a thousand candles. A young woman named Amber said, "I have gained so much understanding and focus from prayer meetings. I realize praying does not change the world overnight, but I continue to believe that someone must be benefiting from my prayers."

Prayer calls attention to ourselves as well as the Father and we benefit from a deepening capacity for discernment and awareness of God's hand in our lives, to distinguish God's intentions from our own, and to decide on the innumerable choices that come into our lives. Our gratitude makes us more pleasing and more centered in the purposes of God, and more generous toward others. This connection brings hospitality toward our family, friends, and the world at large. This hospitality evokes sharing life's burdens, meeting needs, and celebration joys.

We discover and rediscover our need for God and the need for others and their need for us. Appropriate humility is another benefit. We reflect the fullness of God in seeking to imitate Jesus in love. Prayer unites us to all people who seek to follow Jesus. It makes an identifiable difference in the lives of those who pray. Not feeling God's grace that marks our existence and provides freedom for living less encumbered is the cause of additional burdens that come with viewing ourselves as ultimately responsible. We then take on unnecessary spiritual, emotional, and physical burdens. Prayer draws us to God and draws God to us like nothing else. Prayerful eyes see Jesus close-up. Shared faith involves praying for and with another in the presence of God, which increases the intimacy as God's will and purpose come to pass.

Accepting my own existence meaning accepting the relationships that life brings to me and realizing that relationships are gifts. These come because we existed in a particular time and place. My life journey is not in isolation but involves every human that ever lived on this planet. We are interlocked and each plays a part in my finding out who I am as a person. They help or hinder me. If a relationship is wholesome, it will build our community where everything nurtures life. Still I do need some isolated quiet times if my own gifts and contributions is to not become more than superficial. Solitude helps us realize our solidarity with other people. These times of prayer gives us awareness whereby we find a suitable balance between relationships that knit us to other people as well as the solitude needed to nourish the inner parts of those relationships. There are so many benefits of praying. Praying gets us deeper into the Scriptures and the dream of God that we are part of forever. We share an identity with Christ. We develop the fruit of living with ourselves and others as we bear one another's burdens. Reading the Bible requires my interest, attention, and reflection. The same goes for our praying. We cultivate this truth with consistent concentration. We enter a separated place in the presence of God. This is an unique opportunity in the world of demands, questionable values, and life issues that vie for our attention in other places. Praying takes us to a place that makes living faith as our unmatched focus. Our secret place keeps us alert to God and the things of God. We become different because Christ lives inside of us. We share this identity in the redeemed family. My mother used to tell me, "Now Jimmy, don't forget where you came from and who you are." Even as a child and later as a minister, I got the gist of it. As the years went on, I found reasons to hang on to this advice. As I hear people's stories on Facebook, where we can continue to link with so many people with whom we are inseparably linked. We also hooked into where we came from which all lives are unique. Remembering our identity and what informs it from wherever we have lived remains an essential part of our lives. Prayer keeps us attuned to our transformed identity as a base for how we strive to live.

God will wake up every eternal seed planted in our souls. While we are rooted in this earth in this time, place, and space, a part of heaven will blossom into this beautiful truth.

Pray helps us not only to recognize who we are, where we came from, and where we will go. As my mama said, "Prayer prevents us from living as someone we are not. Read Colossians 1:9-12. Prayer brings strength, patience, endurance, and joy. Prayer is so important for nurturing spiritual fruit in ourselves and our friends which becomes the object of our concern. Opening up to the Spirit working in us to allow spiritual fruit to find deeper roots and beautiful blooms. We consider how we act, think, react, feel, and dream. This gives more faith, hope, joy, and love. Prayer brings celebrations and joys through the words of everyone we have ever encountered for those who use the magic of computers to keep in touch. We can share one another's difficulties and rely on persons past and present for support.

Prayer brings the benefit of the joy of companionship with God. Nobody wants to walk the journey of life on each all by themselves. That feeling of wholeness that we just cannot explain. We cherish the moments when God touches our lives with the coming of the morning sun unveiling to us something eternal.

More blessings are in store for us if we will make it an unending time to prayer for others. Prayer makes us able to turn to God to receive what we and others lack, a priceless gift, a wish granted for those who need our spiritual aid. Prayer is a rich and powerful spiritual resource, not an outmoded instrument of a long-vanished piety. In collaboration with the Divine in fulfilling the dream of God by God's activity in the world and in the lives of each of us.

Praying to our merciful maker gifts us to know our needs, our frailties, and faults. We also understand the heavy loads others are carrying with pain. With prayer, we are determined to sow love where we find hate and indifference. It is called compassion for our human family. As we pray for others, it is Jesus the Christ praying for them through us, using our lips, our minds, our hopes to plead before the Father for good things. To pray is to love. To love is to pray. The prayer that has guided my spiritual journey besides the Lord's Model Prayer, is "Make me an instrument of Thy Peace," written and used in a song by Saint Francis of Assisi (1181-1226) founding father of the Franciscans. "Lord, make me an instrument of thy peace,

Where there is hatred, let me sow love.
Where there is injury, pardon.
Where there is doubt, faith.
Where there is despair, hope.
Where there is darkness, light.
Where there is sadness, joy.
O divine Master, grant that I may not so much seek
To be consoled as to console,
To be understood as to understand,
To be loved as to love.
For it is in giving that we receive.
It is in pardoning that we are pardoned.
It is in dying to self that we are born to eternal life.

Heal all that hurts inside, Lord, Until I feel whole and strong, until love and peace abide, Lord, and forgiveness flows along.

~Marjorie Donellen

Chapter Seven

Praying for Forgiveness Brings Healing

Prayer cleans our soul from inner turmoil and anguish, so that we made into rest, wholeness, peace, and joy. When we acknowledge and confess our sinful ways, including all our errors and mistakes, to ourselves and to God, genuine and deep healing begins. Inviting Jesus to come into our human house reminds me of a story that was shared during the winter clergy retreat at Saint Benedict Center. A Lover walked a long distance to go to the house where his Beloved lived. He knocked on her door. The voice inside responded, "Who is there?" The Lover answered, "It is I." The Beloved answered sadly, "There is no room here for both me and you." Giving up the Lover went away and trekked back to his own house. Time passed until the Lover again made the long walk, and again approached the house of his Beloved and knocked. As during his last visit, she said the words, "Who is there?" This time the Lover answered, "It is you." The Beloved opened the door and he was welcomed into the home of the Beloved.

The story could be a parable of God and the human person being clearly separated from one another. As we approach God through grace, we find difficulty in coming to an understanding. We are distinct from God. God is the Lover in this story. Even if divine condescension allows me to achieve some kind of communion with our Lover, we must continue to speak of separateness when we attempt a connection. We must say, "It is I." The parable tells us of the person who has learned to say, "It is You." We attain union with God without effort on our part. Prayer is coming into consciousness of what has always been there. Prayer, silence, and solitude are moments of grace that can awaken us to the possibilities of prayer. We find our true selves in God. Because of this I can discover who I am in God, and I can say, "It is You." Prayer for me is a corrective lens that does away with the distorted view of reality. With some mysterious reason, praying appears to be normal vision, and this corrected vision helps us see what prayer is. God quietly gathers in love the frayed edges where we are living. In our struggle with God for forgiveness, we are like Augustine who prayed, "God make me pure, but not yet." Read II Corinthians 4:16-17. God's dream is to strengthen us in our personal uniqueness concerning our deadness. God calls us to be willing to pray in loving obedience by which we are transformed from death to eternal life.

Forgiveness is a condition in which the sin of the past is not altered. The inevitable consequences are not changed. A fresh act is added to those in the past which restores the broken relationship. The utter blotting out of sin and restoration to wholeness comes in the chamber of our intimate prayers. To be cleansed and to accept the cleansing, we can live as a forgiven one, restored by the gift and grace. As we live before God without ceasing, confessing that we are sinners. We deserve condemnation but in grace, we put away many things that are mere tokens of a pleasure-loving nature. The outer life listens to the inner life. Jesus lives in the inner life, and he grows more and more within us. We feel the attraction that lifts us up from the world. We submit to his love which makes us truly free.

One of the joys of my ministry is my work in prisons and jails. Praying for forgiveness. Basically, when I pray with the unfree, I pray, "Lord of endless hope and joy, we now turn to you in this prison. Lord, listen to the inmates' questions, such as 'Why do we hurt ourselves? Why did we hurt those we love and those who love us? Why did we do those things that we did? As we sink even deeper, unable to deal with feelings when reality makes us aware of the truth. Show my friends in prison the way, give them answers to help them leave this place, and to find new and fulfilling life with you as their healer and savior."

Without forgiveness, life will never change. Look at the nations who harbor only hate. Look at the urban gangs in the United States and all over the world. See our own troubled families. These are places and people who have never known forgiveness. Without forgiveness, all memories of hurting and abusing, rejecting, and hating continues with searing aches and pains. We will only know a continuous duplication of the sufferings in our past in the present moment. A French physician shared *"Tout comprendre c'est tout pardoner,"* which means "To understand all is to forgive all."

Read Romans 8:12-13. Paul was saying if we continue in sin, deadness rules our lives. God touches the deeply ingrained structure of our deadness. By grace we come alive in the image of Christ. Prayer is an act of loving obedience that we offer to God with no strings attached. We pray to change ourselves. Out of a desire to let God make us alive, a conflict occurs, as we tend to fall back into our old ways. Our prayer life must be continuous and be supported by others who share our brokenness and be received with love. When God begins to deal with us in the deep parts of our brokenness, we need others to embrace us in love.

We can ask for forgiveness at any age or stage of life. Resentment burns in souls forever. In the past times, people share about a divorce, a business betrayal, words said to bring hurt to my family. Perhaps through the years, they thought the fire would be extinguished. For decades they waited to hear an apology that never came. Their hurts smolder too long. Forgiveness is difficult even when you are old. They genuinely pray for the cool water of grace to flow until the fire ends.

Forgiveness ultimately sets us free. The act usually comes slowly. We pray to become prepared with a deep willingness to forgive those who have terribly harmed us. This prayer has its own timing. We can pray to be ready. We ask that our hearts will become open and soften as the snows of winter slowly melt, giving life giving water to the parched places we clearly remember. We may never forget the negative experience. Forgiveness never means that we can forget. Forgiving means forgiving those who hurt you, not just accepting or condoning the crime. In forgiveness we know the joy of moving on.

Nothing erodes our serenity than those memories of harm we have done to others. If we are ashamed of something we have done, we will lie about who we are. Our sin brings isolation from those who offer us love and acceptance, including our family, friends, and strangers to whom we have neglected or failed in some harmful way. We tend to keep these sins secret, and we become more wounded, more rejected, more boxed in, shut tightly in our house of fear of being discovered.

Problems with Guilt and Sin

If we are not willing to turn away from sin, we cannot receive the Holy Spirit. Repentance and faith in Jesus are the preconditions. If we turn from sin in our soul and confessed it, we will struggle and suffer dark nights in our souls, but we can receive the spirit. We are not required to be perfect or sinless. Receiving the spirit is a gift to help us overcome sin in our life.

Guilt can be healthy if it leads us to repent, confess, and receive forgiveness. If it is unhealthy—the mafia of our minds—guilt keeps us from God. Given the fullness of the Holy Spirit, we experience the assurance of the love of God and forgiveness.

As we become more intimate with God, we must expose areas of our lives. In every house where I have lived, I had rooms that nobody was allowed to see. These rooms contained a clutter of items that we mostly useless with no order, and often in piles. These rooms were usually in the basement or a dark closet. The rooms reflected my family life. I have kept all my books and sermons, many travel scrapbooks, and tapes and videos of sermons and conferences. Some of us many parts of our lives hidden from being discovered and rejected.

God views our guest rooms. God knocks on one door after another. God exposed rooms I did not know were there. God exposed every dark corner with cleansing light. Give God the run of your house. We are slow to do that. Most hesitate to believe God can be trusted in every area of our lives. Read Proverbs 3:5-6. We do not have to perfect to deserve the love of God. We are ashamed of our imperfections. We hide our shortcomings. Secret fears can keep us from the serenity we need. When we pray to be forgiven, we are asking God to set us free from hiding, pretense, and shame. We want the joy of being fully accepted for who we are. For that to happen, we must be willing to give God the right-of-way by praying, "Jesus, be the Lord over every area of my life." In our soul house, God simple knocks persistently and quietly. Jesus never said to anybody, "you are untouchable to me, or that we are too far gone, too poor and smelly, and our circumstances are that we are too dead to enliven. God will breathe life into all the dead places in our house. Nothing could ever help God fulfill the dream of healing our souls. This is a long act of our will. When Jesus taught us how to pray, he said, "Forgive our trespasses or debts," he presumed that we would sin against our sisters and brothers. None of us can say that we have never brought harm to another.

We are selfish, angry, frustrated, and we say many unkind things. We tell small white lies. We take things that do not belong to us. We take advantage of other people for our own personal gain. Each one has an inexhaustible capacity for imperfection. When we ask God to forgive our sins, we are prepared to confess, honestly, openly, uncomfortably, within our essential humanity. The root of confession is "to reveal and declare our identity." We confess sins that are public as well as those that are private. Whenever we forgive or are forgiven, it is like throwing open the windows and allowing in fresh air and light.

We come to God with assurance that God will not use our confessed sins to hurt us anymore. God will not love us less because of our admissions. There will be no ridicule for confessed sin. There are no limits or restrictions on God's forgiveness. Read Psalm 103:12, Jeremiah 31:34, and I John 1:9. The baggage of keeping up appearances is relinquished. We let down our guard and tell the truth. The result will be warm love in return. Concealing the sins we do in our secret places prevents us drinking deep from the healing grace and unconditional forgiveness. Most of the many books on prayer none do more to show its reasonableness than the ones I read by old authors found in Yale Divinity School and other places. John Killinger taught a class on prayer in the D.Div. program of Preaching, Worship, and Literature. His books are brilliant.

Alcoholics Anonymous is among the most far reaching spiritual healing group. Addicts diligently work to heal the anguish through a program of recovery. AA is based on twelve steps. Most of these steps indicate that our deepest need rests in our capacity to address unacknowledged shortcomings in our own lives. Some of my clients and parishioners say they are "spiritual but not religious." Some addicted people would say that I could not help them because I was not an alcoholic. I assured them had to conquer my own addictions that had the same roots as their addiction. Seven of the twelve steps target our willingness to recognize, admit, and correct the ways we destroy ourselves. Read the Twelve Steps in an Alcoholics Anonymous basic book. Jesus told us not to judge others. He insisted on our need to take a personal inventory of our own sins. He said, "First take the log out of your own eye, that you may see more clearly the splinter in your brother or sister's eyes. At Valley Hope Addictions Treatment Centers in Lincoln and Omaha, therapists sat with clients to do a moral inventory. Counselors had done their treatment assessment before the entered into the Valley Hope program. There was nothing they could tell us that surprised us.

Blessings Despite Our Sins

My confessing prayer times are mostly communicated in private. Going to see a therapist or a trusted friend. Jesus insisted we all have sinned. To sin is to miss the mark. We get off center. Every day in scores of ways, we miss the mark. We are human beings and missing the mark is what we all do. If missing the mark has harmed you, forgive yourself. If your sins harm another person, ask for their forgiveness. Confession brings awareness and a more accurate and loving way to live. That's where repentance comes in. To repent is to turn around in a new direction, to begin again. Repentance is not an option. Our sin ripples out into the world, or the sin will grow in unexpected ways. In confession, we receive the healing balm of the Next Place.

God hears our confession. We feel the memory of how we brought harm to another. I have dreamed about the consequences of my harming others. And I see the faces of those who have harmed me. My body tightens around the heart. You remember and see the videos of your sins. God enfolds us in safety and love. We speak our confession of our sin and see where it continues to live in the tissues of our body. We are then forgiven as we feel a weight lifted. As we are forgiven, we must forgive others. Forgiving sets us free. In leading a congregation to find the powerful sacrament of forgiveness, we shared places and times when some have been abused or hurt. Those gashes of woundedness runs deep and the constant videos in the mind scared the body, mind, and soul. Forgiving others is indispensable for spiritual freedom. Forgiveness from God comes with our forgiving those who sin against us. If we refuse to do our part, we cut ourselves off from God's part. Jesus insists that we not even approach the altar of communion or prayer without first resolving any hurt or conflict with the one whom we sinned against. The unwillingness to forgive lessons our capacity for nourishment and liberation that we seek in prayer. Forgiveness takes time, courage, and compassion. Being forgiven and forgiving is an invitation to be set free, to walk unencumbered into the household of heaven.

Jesus invites us to the same love and mercy that God has shown for us. We forgive others not only for their good but for ours. The path of forgiveness is the only road away from past sins and hurts. God will give us the power to forgive. How could people forgive the Nazis who killed millions and used their power and German economic failure to get people to join in their evil? We can only imagine. They had made Adolph Hitler their savior. How God must have cried as young Nazi soldiers wore "God be with us" on their uniform belts and prayed for the Nazi nationalism that aimed to rule the world. During eight trips to preach in Germany, I could not imagine the friendly and clean, beautiful, and prosperous citizens of Germany believing and acting on the propaganda of the Nazi administration. A German Lutheran pastor said, "Forgiveness is the only healing pathway for the horrid past. God's power to forgive is stronger than the power of hate to get even." He then shared the story of Corrie Ten Boom whose father and sister died in Nazi concentration camps. One Sunday as she was sharing about forgiveness in a Dutch church, she actually met a former Nazi guard who had done so much evil to her. She said her intimacy with God in prayer gave her the strength to forgive that man and to become free from the pain of the past.

The healing power of God is at work within us even now. Be assured that Jesus walks with us. There is light at the end of this life tunnel filled with darkness. Jesus holds the light of faith for us now. He will hold his lamp as long as it is needed, until you are ready to carry a loving light for yourself.

I have enjoyed the teaching and books on prayer by Dr. John Killinger and Richard Foster. I did profit from reading Fosdick and Buttrick on prayer.

Sit in your secret place. In your own way of praying, allow the image of someone who has hurt you to arise in your mind. You could even look at a photograph. Be gentle and patient with yourself. Allow your words to be spoken slowly. With those haunting memories, you may resist forgiveness which is human and natural. Try to be merciful and kind. Perhaps you can say something like: "For all that you have done that caused me pain through your words and actions, I forgive you. I forgive you now. I forgive you. I set you free. And I set myself free from you and the harm you did to me. Amen." You may have to have more times of prayer before you sense relief and freedom. Forgiveness takes time and courage. In your intimate praying, you will know the joy that forgiveness always gives to you. Prayer is the key. Read James 5:15-16. Christian congregations are good at telling us that we ought to pray, but not nearly so effective at telling us how. In all my situations in leading churches to have a prayer meeting, we have more than 500 average attendance, but just two or three for a prayer meeting. We know that prayer does heal. All of us can think of examples. There are so many.

When I served as associate superintendent of Buchanan Boys Home in Saint Joseph, Missouri, we had a boy with an unrestrainable impulse toward violence. He had wrecked his family home, terrorized his sisters and his mom. He was expelled from school numerous times. He had beat up a teacher. We did physical activities, privilege limitations, anything. Finally, when he came into the counseling office, I prayed with him. After much struggle, the delinquent boy changed. He quieted down. Somehow, he chose not to use his anger and violence.

In a reform institution where miracles were in short supply, when emotional problems remain unsolved, the prayer was not wasted. Hate and attitudes and unforgiveness might prevail. Still, I learned from loving those boys, that problems such as their difficulties can become unexpected opportunities. The world needs all of us in the helping professions to become prayer therapists. Prayer is God's anointed way by which we become channels of healing power.

My friend Scott Taylor published his written prayers in a book titled *Seasons of Prayer*. He served as minister of the First Christian Church in Grand Island, Nebraska. I recommend his prayers. He told me, "Jim, you taught me that joy is infectious . . . in the best way." Let me close this book with Scott's prayer, based on Mark 1:4-11, called, "I Am Forgiven." The water is chilly and it shocks my breathe away. I have nothing to hold onto Except your grace, O God! Will you be there Again …. And again? Blessed Spirit Fill me with your loving Touch and sweet perfume. My heart knows joy and it is as if Heaven broke open and you wrapped me gently in your soft arms. I am forgiven. Forgiven to be able to feed my friends, to be able to feed the stranger. Forgiven to be able to love my neighbor and let them be just Who they are. Forgiven to be able to face this morning and tomorrow morning and the next one after that.

The water is chilly but Your love and quiet voice Warm me and comfort me. Now I am your child. Thank you, God. Thank you. (Scott Taylor, *Seasons of Prayer,* pp. 40-41)

"Love one another as I have loved you." (John 15:12) Jesus' love is our resource. Our love is made possible in response to his love. His costly forgiveness is our source. Our resource is a response to his forgiveness.

By God's grace and saving power, when life has hurt us, we are able to respond with forgiveness. Praying for forgiveness will change your life. It is the glorious pathway to healing. We can in confidence pray, "Thank you Jesus, that your will is to free me from the evil of unforgiveness. Let your will be done."

Don't ever underestimate the capacity of a human being who is determined to do something.

~Edna Ismail

Chapter Eight

Discovering Our Calling in Intimate Prayer

I was born on a Tuesday in May. The following Sunday, I was enrolled in the cradle roll of the First Baptist Church in Kingsport, Tennessee. Before my birth, my mother prayed that God would use me as a pastor. My dad enlisted in the Army during World War II. During my childhood, I was brought to Sunday School at Woodlawn Baptist Church. I was baptized at the age of eight. I enjoyed hearing about Jesus. I enjoyed learning how to read and write.

We find God's calling at we look at episodes in our lives. Prayer unveils a blessing and an awareness of context in our lives. Paying attention to the memories brings deep intimate insight about ourselves and God. Relax and open yourself to reexperiencing the difficult and challenging times and the joyful ones. Memory of a past event might be nagging you. As Minister of Joy to the world, I know I find the experiences of joy so wonderful, I want to relive them. Be sensitive to the tastes, smells, touches, sights, and hearing in your memory. Try to sort out how God was there with you. With this gift of intimate prayer, we listen to the Holy Spirit's movement through our emotions, our thoughts, and bodily reactions. This makes our own choices in line with the Spirit, as we discover in prayer how God desires us to act. Hindsight rather than foresight as we sift through all the possibilities of where we might serve. The choices we make affects the context of life. Who you marry, where you decide to work, when you beget children, causes your life to be free or in a place that gives you Hell on earth? Use your intuition and imagination to think of yourself as full of years looking back on your responses, and perhaps wishing what you had done. To reclaim our history means that we no longer relate to our past as years in which only good times are remembered. When we are truly ready to discover our calling, the joy of salvation brings the freedom to find a vocation as in praying our entire lives is the source of energy that moves us into the future. Prayer bids our humanity at full stretch before the One who calls us.

Little has survived my childhood. I have some rocks from places I visited, some marbles, stamps from my stamp collection, a few baseball cards, old school report cards, and some photos of football and basketball history from newspapers and books.

I still have reminders of my youth. I have my first sermon, "Sermon Preached on a Football Field," delivered before a football game between Haynesfield School and the Royal Ambassadors' team from church. There are still photographs of playing like Indian fighting with backyard forts and my old baseball mitts. I had stacks of comic books. I read them while hunched under my bedroom covers with my flashlight. Carnivals, circuses, and rodeos were annual entertainment. I read books from the old Bristol Public Library, looked at world maps, received Boy Scout badges from my Boy Scout Troop 8, and saved the medal pins from the Ridgecrest Baptist Assembly, programs from Tennessee High School, the University of Tennessee, and Shaw Stadium, home of the class D professional Bristol Twins. I cherish all these things because they brought me so much joy. I see videos of playing hide and seek, biking around the block, playing sandlot sports in vacant fields, playing church, playing with yoyos, marble tournaments on a non-grassed field where we drew circle and marbles placed, as we used the steelies to knock marbles out of the ring, selling pop bottles out of little red wagons, spinning tops, sledding down the hill on the left side of the hill, go carts built with our dads, and mowing lawns. It was like a Soap Box Derby coasting down Jonesboro Road.

During those days of endless play, I got into my share of mischief and naughty things. Sometimes I got caught red-handed or tattled on, mostly by my brothers. The methods my parents used to deal with this was not prayer, but washing my mouth out with soap, hitting me with a switch or belt. My parents would say that my body was a temple of the Holy Spirit, or we punish you because we love you. One Sunday afternoon my brother Ed was whacked hard with my dad's belt. In church worship you were not allowed to say a word unless the pastor asked you something during his sermon.

One Sunday, I was caught off guard when the pastor said, "Jimmy, what do the birds do." I answered that birds fly, birds eat warms, birds sing songs. Pastor looked at me and said, "Birds flock together." My brother was guilty of talking during church worship. That was a cultural sin. Getting into fights during grade school was always anticipated and expected. I took a hard fist now and then, and I slugged others. I never started a fight. I never picked on anyone or bullied them. Families left their home doors unlocked or open. Nobody took anything that belonged to others. Everybody went to church. Most got saved at early ages. There were no gangs or drugs. The annual Bristol Preaching Mission brought crowds of people from every denomination into one place. Prayers, Bible reading, and other religious activity was shared.

I believe God places us in the world in a certain time and place to complete the purpose he has for each person. One of the most important results you bring into the world is the you that you really want to be. An interest is something that draws you. A skill is something that you learn to do. An experience is an emotional or mental perception that you have possess, or a physical thing you have accomplished. A gift is what you are born with and that God gives you like hearts beating and breathing. In our Puritan backgrounds, we focus on what we are not good at doing. No wonder we think something is wrong with us. To create a work that you love and is within the will of God, pay attention to what feeds and nourishes your soul. Focus on what you have felt most satisfied doing regardless of what others have said you should feel. "Do you really want to be happy? You start by being appreciative of who you are and what you've got." said Pooh. Bing intimate with God is to discover the joys of your own journey. What all of us can do for those we care about is to listen to them, love them, be there for them, pray for their best, and do the work God has called you to show each one their own pathway.

After I received a degree in English literature at Carson-Newman University, I knew that I wanted to be trained to write, not just writing a dissertation on some poem or thesis like the ones I briefed through at the Browning Armstrong Library at Baylor University. I chose to get training from the best and oldest journalism school in the world, the University of Missouri in Columbia.

While I was still considering my call to become a pastor, I served as editor for the *Midwestern Spire*. My journey has taken me to study more than 20 years in seminaries. Again, I wanted to train at the best place, so I chose to attend Vanderbilt University Divinity School.

My sense of where and how and where I would share the joy of my salvation with the world was not in the seminary. Poring over dusty volumes of theology, church history or solving exegetical problems in Hebrew and Greek made me sense that I was not feeling joy in this area. I continued to search. Finally, I earned the Doctor of Psychology degree and wrote my dissertation on *Integration of Joy* in *Family Counseling* at the University of Oxford. I have always enjoyed my gifts of research and writing academic volumes.

One of my most interesting and challenging work was as a writer and public relations specialist for the Sunday School Board of the Southern Baptist Convention. While serving there I enjoyed writing hundreds of articles and did radio and television programs such as a program on the Asheville station with guests who were presenters at Ridgecrest Baptist Assembly. I enjoyed spending summers in beautiful western North Carolina. I wrote volumes for Baptist Press, secular presses, and articles on all the college age staff members for their home newspapers. Although I was sought by Southern Baptist state papers to serve as an associate editor and for the news magazine for the North Carolina Children's Home in Thomasville. I kept my workaholic search, finished my doctorate at Vanderbilt in preaching, worship, and literature. I next accepted a call to serve as pastor for the East Side Baptist Church, an American Baptist congregation in Evansville, Indiana. I did not expect the impossible job that comes from serving as a pastor.

I found joy as a writer, not as a therapist or a pastor. And if I had listened and surrendered myself to God's loving direction and appreciate the things that brought me joy, I would have known that. And I would have known this a long time ago if I'd only been alert to God's dream for me. I often skipped the hallways of childhood and youth, stopping at times to catch my breath. I should have had more honest counseling after I went down the aisle at the summer Royal Ambassador youth camp in Erwin, Tennessee to make public my call to preach. I never got a glimpse of the reality of the organized church. The "call" filled my lungs with refreshing air and my soul with hopeful dreams.

Nothing is sadder than to observe an aimless life. That person aims at many passing things, not with permanent things. She is changeable, unstable, and uncertain. Gifts are used for unworthy purposes. Many lives are brilliant failures. These unsteady ones strive after things that they were never intended to do. Some reasonable people never ask why they were placed on this earthly journey. God has equipped us with every gift of our human nature and grace for mind, body, and gifts needed. No one is more fit to do her chosen work. We tend to envy others' gifts, so we try to do something more to our taste or a job that is showier. Admiring the gifted preachers, I was discontent if I did not find an opportunity to be like other famous preachers. For most of us, doors are closed in the beginning. We feel shut out from various positions and spheres of influence that ambition and pride have led us into. God has never withheld anything in a grudging spirit because our will would be in the way.

Remember, the call of God to whatever, may be a call to conversion This call opens our eyes to see purpose and will of God through ordinary events and experience of life. God cares for our happiness now. Everything that affects us is of interest to God. None of our prayers will move God. Troubles, blessings, temptations, opportunities will come. Each enables our best selves We see the will of God in little events as we exercise our faith. That means for us to keep our wills free until we know the will of God. During the times of waiting, the will accepts what it could not have accepted. Many of us do wishing not willing. Wishing is natural. Wishes causes us to become anxious. Wills act in opposition to the wishes for growth and strength. Despite the obstacles within and without Love is the pathway of our journey to fulfill the purpose of God.

Praying for your life's work involves the most important part of your life's journey. We do not pray so we will be successful and honored with fame. Our goal is not to acquire money, but to realize our part in the dream of God. God is concerned about our work. I am sure that it grieves God to see millions lose jobs because of the worldwide pandemic virus.

Intimately sharing the joys and the problems of working in the world of greedy owners and bad bosses who can make life miserable, is so vital. Pray for help in the immediate job or the lifelong calling. Always thank God for the privilege of having employment. Allow God to speak to your soul about ways of approaching whatever you do. Meaninglessness gives way to laughter, to an exciting pathway, to intimate companionship with God and others, to a reborn delight in living in God's will.

I think the Holy Spirit wanted me to share all this to help you my readers to find what finding your vocation could involve. God calls our name in patient, accepting, tolerating, loving ways. Until recently, looking back at my life and work, I know I never fully understood being so loved by God. God was calling me by my true name. God will tell us who we are. We will all be shown what we could do if only we have the eyes to see and ears to hear, and the willingness to know where we came from and the humility to accept our place in the kingdom of God.

The unseen witnesses are all around us. As long as God leaves us here on earth, there is something we are meant to do, and as we do it, God helps us find the strength, the courage, the acceptance, and grace, all we need.

Walking in nature is a perfect backdrop to combine exercise, prayer, and meditation as calming rituals while enhancing the benefit of these activities.

~Chuck Norris

Chapter Nine

Prayer and the Joy of Sensuality

Prayer is the ongoing practice of sharing my past, present, and future in intimacy with God. We change the images we have of God. During prayer meetings we change our understandings about God. Jurgen Moltman, a professor at Yale Divinity School, said, "When I love God, I love the beauty of bodies, the rhythm of movements, the shining of eyes, the feelings, the scents, the sounds of creation."

We tend to think that we "have" bodies rather than realize that we "are" bodies. Engaging our bodies in prayer brings new experiences. Loving God with the body helps us not feel awkward or uncomfortable about what we look like. People who connect with God in body prayer feel the intimacy in muscles, not just the brain. God walks, breathes, and stretches with us. In our Hebrew classes, we are taught the meaning of the word "*ruach*" is translated spirit, wind, or breath. During the pandemic of the virus, we were made aware of people dying, suffering from lack of ability to breathe. Breathing is a life-sustaining action. As we notice the lungs moving in and out, God intermingles with our spirit, we are enlivened as we permit our body to exhale slowly. Seek relaxed yet intentional focus. If you feel like this is a struggle, remember God is Spirit who breathes with you in prayer.

A. J. Beaber is an extraordinary woman of beauty and joy. She leads conferences and directs women in the area of spirituality and sexuality. She and I have been friends for several years. She wrote the forward to my book, *The Silence of the Church: The Spiritual Struggle with Sexuality*. She authored a special book with the title *You & I, Inc.*, which is a novel about young women's experiences and developing stages in her sexual life. Her novel and my book reveal sexuality as a gift from God. When we practice intimacy in prayer, we taste, see, smell, and hear the love of God. Human sexuality brings pleasure. Anything with a bodily focus— eating, drinking, holding, hugging—causes our bodies to feel life at a new level.

Intimacy is falling in Love. The most insightful literature on prayer is erotic. Charles Wesley sang, "Jesus, Lover of my soul." Prayer is about an enduring, growing, continuing love relationship.

In my book about the silence of the church, I react to the abuses that people perform such as sex trafficking, ignorance, using another person, sexual sin by pastors and priests, especially after so much media consideration of the horrible reality.

Our sensual experiences such as listening to music, writing a book, painting an art piece, playing sports and exercise, sign language, and other experiences gives connection to God who loves us. A.J. Beaber says she enjoys pole dancing as she enjoys her created body. She articulates the connection between sexuality and spirituality in her Thursday Night Thoughts presentations. She believes that if we honor God with our sensuality, we can also know God through our sexuality. Women and men who listen to her podcasts that creates a place for being comfortable speaking about sex at church or in the bedroom. In prayer we sense God around us and in us, and often we feel warm sexual feelings. The church and my community were silent. During one of Dr. Norman Vincent Peale's Schools of Practical Christianity, I experienced a workshop on prayer. The leader was a stance conservative United Methodist minister. He asked participants to share when they know God in a deep way. I said, "When I enjoy sex with my wife, I am aware of God and his love." The group leader's body turned red, and he quickly turned toward others. Sometimes the church teaches us that sex is wrong. With our false guilt, we try to stop praying in our sensuality, we only share with God things in our minds.

God views human sexuality as more than sexual gratification or genital sex. We continue to be sexual our entire lives. People are sexual when they are young or old, sick, or well, single or coupled, sexually alive or celibate. Sexuality is God's gift, calling us out of separation, selfishness, and loneliness into communion and loving communication. In my book about the silence of the church, I attempted to concretely and imaginatively show the connection of praying with our bodies in an incarnational exploration. My purpose in my writing was to speak out about the abuses of God's gift.

Intimacy with God means falling in love. Sexual delight intensifies the yearning for a joyous union of another kind. Prayer may begin with an emptiness, an awareness that sensuality cannot touch where we hurt. Sex will only tease us with hints that joy that needs no justification than the heart of the experience. Praying in the Spirit is a flame of divine love that sets afire with its intoxication. Augustine confessed, "You have made us for yourself, Lord, and our heart can find no rest until it rests in you." On earth we cherish joy in hope, and in the Next Place, complete joy in fulfillment of our hope. In our living in Love, Joy is so precious delightful that we go on glorifying God which is an enjoyment forever.

Now I need to give you a word of caution least you become confused. Your new understandings about intimacy with God in no way means that all sexual thoughts lead us closer to God. Not every sexual experience is sacred or spiritual. Pleasure seekers are distracted by fantasy, sexual imaginings, and self-centered thoughts, rather than the experience of being loved totally by God. Misplaced fantasy or sexual addiction take the focus away from God. Denying our sexuality will not protect us from sin. We must be aware of the danger of injuring our souls. Desire and Sexual Sin Any female-male relationship involves some creative tension is heightened by the feelings of being drawn compellingly by sexual desire.

Marital love delights in faithful intimacy. Marital sensuality mirrors God's love and faithfulness that love creates. Spiritual friendships become a relationship of lovers. It becomes an unsatisfactory substitute for another kind of love. Hiding behind the mask of unspoken expectations, there is a danger as we imagine who else is in the picture. Harboring hopes to which the other cannot respond causes the union to be jeopardized. If the ideal conditions of friendship are met, there is always a crucible of communication between all involved. There is difficulty in loving someone intimately and not be able to express that intimacy in its fulness. Love cries out for consummation.

In the Bible, Paul says, "in Christ there is neither male nor female." That truth does not mean one's sexuality is erased, but the sexes are not divided against each other but gathered together in their full distinctiveness in equality between people. Spiritual friendship between a female and a male is a type of relationship in which the language of love and death, desire, and darkness, provides boundaries and direction. The love that is shared is within the gift of opening up in a desire for intimacy and at the same time they relinquish the possibility of full intimacy of their gift to one another and to the wider community. This is rare Christian friendship that is a sign of hope in a world starved for love that is embraced with joy. With that context, we live in the freedom of God's unbelievable love.

Passionate love is the subject of a small book placed in the middle of our Holy Scriptures. It can be seen as the extreme bodily union with God. Churches have neglected teaching or preaching from the Song of Songs as for centuries church leaders felt so uncomfortable with this erotic love poem. Read the Song of Solomon in its entirety. Read the writer's affirmation of the goodness of sexuality. Feel the range of the beautiful words as a church or community group takes turn reading. See the connection between love of friends and family is like the divine-human relationship. God's passionate love for us comes because the joy of sex is holy. As we long for intimacy with our Lover God, we desire human companionship. The people in your circles may not be aware of it, but with God, you are a spiritual explosion waiting to happen.

A young nurse and gifted athlete from Nebraska shared how see found closeness with God as she ran on a trail. She was a cheerleader and played basketball and volleyball in college and high school.

A Prayer Walk is a way to connect. With others I have walked through a town where I am sharing the joy of the Lord. During critical times, we have walked around the State Capitol Building in Lincoln, Nebraska, stopping to join in prayers, singing, and preaching from the steps of this important place. This is body and prayer in motion. It is walking in the light of love. What joy and refreshment come in the gentle rhythm of your breathing, your stride, and your heartbeat.

There are many labyrinths in the lawns or near churches everywhere. It is a winding path that leads ultimately to the center. There you breathe in God's spirit and turn around and walk through the circles to the beginning point. I always choose to walk slowly. If you encounter someone like me walking at a different walking pace, feel free to walk around them with gentle respect and grace.

The ultimate dream for us is constant, the divine strategy of reaching that goal may be swiftly and joyously altered in the light of the occurrence of the prayers of committed women and men.

I enjoy staying in monasteries as I travel. I join in praying for the entire world. During this Covid-19 pandemic, monks are consistent in their daily existence. These sacred communities have always fascinated me. I love to visit in the ancient ones filled with mystery, where reclusive monks have been praying for hundreds of years. The Gregorian chants bring a sense of commitment and devotion as they have in spiritual solitude with prayer connections that keep them in intimate joy as they fall deeper in love with God. I enjoyed the newer ones such as the Charterhouse of the Transfiguration, located in the area in southern Vermont near Mount Equinox.

This unimaginably beautiful place was built in 1970. Cloistered brothers live in that only Carthusian monastery in North America. They live in silence and work in community. The Carthusians were founded in 1084 by Saint Bruno. In 2020, there are an estimated 400 monks and nuns living on three continents. The Vermont complex includes buildings of mysterious stone and concrete set against the dark wooded mountains. Loons sing around the clear ponds that reflect the sky on sunny days. The sky turns with colors included a baby spanked pink. The air is always unpolluted, laced with pine and stirrings of unseen life.

Travel will become more limited in coming years. The praying monks will tell you that you really have no need to travel anywhere. We have come to realize that we can enjoy God right where we live, in any place where God and the servant hold frequent conversations as between friends. Praying means listening and speaking. Silence and solitude are conducive to being deeper into God. In more and more congregations, we are told there is more listening since the endemic virus has forced us to use Zoom or You-Tube for worship. Few are involved in the worship preparation. Few are there face to face with the preacher. Some churches estimate doubling their attendance since the winter of 2020. We can drink tea or coffee, enjoy breakfast, or stay in bed. Our living spaces have become cathedrals. We do not resist, but just remain still. Sensuality in a wooded forest brings glimpses of heaven that we might never see. We hear God's still small voice more clearly. We smell the freshness. We taste Jesus' body in common mealtimes. We find an intimacy in prayer beyond the senses. The Kingdom of Joy has arrived on earth.

There are many things that are essential to arriving at the true peace of mind, and one of the most important is faith, which cannot be acquired without prayer.

~John Wooden

Chapter Ten

Prayer as a Healing Word

Medical students are astounded with the countless number of things that can go wrong with any human being. In the beginning, student doctors see illness everywhere. Numerous things do go wrong. Sometimes illness comes in complete surprise. The world is now praying and facing a pandemic virus. One afternoon in Wytheville, Virginia, I visited an older woman who was suffering with terminal cancer. As I sat in a chair by her bed, she talked about her trust in Jesus. She told the story of a time in years past when she was seriously ill. She was prayed for by a former pastor. Unexpectedly, she made a remarkable recovery. She was certain the healing came from prayer. She did not get a physical healing. We had prayed for healing. Against all odds, we prayed for a miracle with a surge of life here and now. In her death and in trusting Jesus, there will be another surge of spiritual life for her forever in the Next Place.

Those who suffer from serious illness know how difficult it is to pray. While you are suffering, it appears impossible to have any spark of energy, motivation, or interest in praying. God seems so far away. It seems useless to get God's attention. While you are suffering, you may just not be able to pray. You think that God has betrayed you. There might be days you desire to pray, and other days you are angry with God.

Healing is the point of convergence in the dream of God that becomes reality in human life. Healing is the main pathway to knowledge of God. Healing comes about through the action of the living Christ within us. In my ministry of pastoral psychotherapy with clients exhibiting varying degrees of mental health, I believe That a deficiency of love is at the center of most of human troubles. We need to love and to be loved. This was the theme of my book, *Passionate Joy*. As we journey toward God, our souls seek deep, loving, intimate relationships with other human beings. We live in at a time of isolation and broken hearts. From the day of our conception in our mother's womb, the most significant force for shaping lives is love. That love, as life-giving and full of wonder cannot heal our suffering inner child deprived by others. God's healing power reaches the inner child to bring wholeness and freedom. Jesus does not erase the memory of the pain. The secrets in our heart dwell in the darkness of shame. We survive with broken bodies but not with broken spirits. God does not will sickness, pain, or suffering.

Pray as you can, not as you can't. Prayers of an ill one sit quietly as the seeker in the stillness is waiting for God. There is no right and wrong way to pray. Praying is allowing God to share in our healing. Developing intimate and consistent praying makes a pathway for God to be your companion to enter into your suffering, to share your pain, and to raise you to a new life.

The leading diagnosis in physician office visits is hypertension with respiratory infection and bronchitis. We are all going to be sick, injured, or ill during our time on earth. Some will be much sicker than others. Trips to the doctor and hospitalization are harbingers of our ultimate deaths. Emotional disorders affect millions, not because they lack character or weakness of will.

In our prayer groups, we pause to consider the people within our influence. Do you know people suffering from a debilitating physical illness? What about those struggling with heart disease or cancer? Substance abuse? Domestic violence?

Holy Scripture tells of brokenness which indicates we all need some kind of healing. Prayer is the healing salve for opening our bodies to the healing touch of our intimate God. The healing ministry of Jesus is recorded throughout the synoptic gospels. Most of the healing narratives address issues that transcend physical aspects. The healing word reveals Jesus' attempts to restore the whole person. Half of the stories deal with marginalized people in society now and then. Jesus' healing word healed lepers, demon-possessed, women suffering from incurable diseases, and those racially discriminated against by the Jews and Romans. We have discussed the message of salvation, including forgiveness, and the understanding of faith. Jesus' healing did not focus on a single dimension of healing, but to bring people into intimate wholeness.

The healing word of Jesus helps us understand that healing was the hallmark of his ministry. Wherever Jesus went, people brought the sick to him. And he healed thousands. During his time on earth, his preaching, teaching, and healing caused his popularity. New about him spread across the lands. They came with various diseases, those suffering in severe pain, those having seizures, and the paralyzed, and he healed them. Unbelievably large crowds followed him from Galilee, Decapolis, Jerusalem, Judea, and regions across the Jordan River sought his word of healing.

After John the Baptist was put in prison, he sent some of his disciples to Jesus to find out whether Jesus was the Messiah. John did this because his ministry differed so much from John's ministry. John and Jesus' ministries both had a foundational word, "Repent for the Kingdom of God is at hand. (Matthew 3:2, 4:17) Jesus' word for John's disciples was "Go back and report to John what you hear and see. The blind receive sight, the lame walk, those who have leprosy are cured." (Matthew 11:4-5)

Jesus wanted the Jewish leadership to realize that he was the Messiah. Those religious men had all the knowledge. They had the rules necessary to keep Jewish tradition. Jesus' healing ministry demonstrated his divinity. His deep desire was for the rabbis to realize that he was the fulfillment of their Messianic hopes. Jesus possessed the intuitive insight that healing was a sure way to capture their attention with dramatic healing.

In times like these with people dying from the pandemic, we are more aware of how people suffer from so many ailments and deadly diseases. Sickness affects more than the physical dimension. It affects the whole person: body, mind, emotions, spirituality, and community. When a person is sick, they cannot function to their maximum capacity. They will be less productive at tasks needed to do.

Sickness is not part of the dream of God. Sin is what causes us to be susceptible to its illness. Sin affects the whole person. Jesus is the essential way God planned for the whole of humanity to be reconciled back to God.

Christians look at the healing ministry of Jesus from a physiological or biological perspective. They pray that God will intervene as they face physical illness. When intervention does not happen, people become discouraged. Jesus' word for healing meant more than the restoration of physical health. What can we learn from the purpose of Jesus' ministry?

Most of the stories of healings performed by Jesus as written in the gospels, address issues that go beyond mere physical healing. They point us to the importance of wholeness.

There are 22 stories about healing in the synoptic Matthew-Mark-Luke accounts. Fifteen of those narratives tell stories of Jesus' ministry to the poor and marginalized. They include lepers, beggars, women, demon possessed, and those cruelly discriminated against during the days of Jesus' time. Jesus' word in his healing work included the issues of sin and salvation, as in the story of the paralytic. He addressed the role of faith. Some of the accounts deal with for the most part the physical issues in healing. A closer reading includes dimensions other than physical aspects of healing.

We are going to suffer. We must remember that no matter how often we pray, the kind of prayers we pray, or how prayerfully we live, we will all die. It is healthy and fruitful to look at life from the perspective of our ultimate physical death. Problems and troubles become clearer as we think about what we want life experiences to be like. No matter what happens, no matter how many miraculous healings, our bodies will not be physically healed. Lazarus was raised from the dead, but he did not go on living forever.

It is difficult to quiet down, to focus, to concentrate. The mind races. The body is tense and restless. John Killinger and others who give guidance on preparing for prayer. Play some soothing music. Relax the tension and stress in your body. Let go of the distractions in your mind. Breathing in, breathing out, you let your mind and body settle.

Evelyn Underhill said, "When you can't hold on to God, God is holding you." Jesus invites you to a precious intimacy with him in times of suffering. Jesus is living within you. You have many Christians as they share faith with each other. Let Jesus embrace you. The deepest reality of life is the many ways God loves us.

Failure to be healed is not God letting us down. Putting ourselves at the center is not changing anything. Paul lived with his thorn in the flesh, and with ultimate joy, we did not turn angry, bitter, or negative. We all suffer, die, and all influenced by evil forces. The evil one has left a mark. No one is perfect and whole. We are broken. God makes a way out of our dark brokenness. Paul insists that he lived with a changed perspective. He boasts about his weaknesses that makes him stronger. He is telling us that we can yield to a higher power. Jesus can be leaned upon in our weaknesses. The best way to pray is the way we pray best. Take everything exactly as it is. Put it all in God's hands and leave it to God.

Dietrich Bonhoeffer shared, "Make room for all that which is capable of rejoicing, enlarging, or calming your heart."

There is difficulty that healing sought may not happen. We want our affliction to go away. Saint Paul tells us, he pleaded with God three times for the thorn to be removed. The ailment remained. When we enjoy an intimate relationship with God, so when we encounter an affliction, the first thing we need to do is pray. Physical healing may not take place, but a deeper healing will be our lot.

Our health will fail us. Our circumstances will cause us stress. Loving God despite our sin and brokenness, God's power is complete.

Jesus spoke to the issue of sabbath keeping in Matthew 12:1-14, when he healed a man with a withered hand. In Luke 14:1-6, he cured a man of dropsy. These two accounts give evidence of the laws of the Pharisees were spiritual blinding them as to the issue of healing.

Physically, Jesus wanted to heal both men of their illnesses. He was keenly aware that the religious rulers put much emphasis on sabbath rules. The healed men were liberated to understand God's creative power and love. Jesus was teaching those Pharisees who were watching him. He demonstrated for the people of his time that healing a human being was more important than a bunch of man- made rules and rituals.

As I prepared for a Healingquest for Saint Elizabeth Regional Medical Center in Lincoln, I saw that faith is emphasized in nine of the twenty-two accounts of healing with Jesus. Without these healing accounts, we would not realize how essential faith is the matrix for physical healing. Faith was so important that Jesus could heal without being present with the person who sick, but faith made them whole. Read Matthew 8.

Jesus asked the ill ones, "Do you have faith that I can do this?" And he would say "Do you believe I am able to do this?" Jesus telling them to trust in him for spiritual wholeness through his healing. Healing brought into view the joy of practicing the presence of God. Jesus' healings were intimately tied to his role as savior. Healing made clearer his mission. Jesus performed many other miracles such as turning water into wine and walking on water. Mark reports that wherever Jesus traveled "they laid the sick in the marketplaces and begging him that they might touch even the fringe of his clock; and all who touched it were healed." (Matthew 5:25-34)

Without faith, Jesus could not heal. In Matthew 13:58, we read:" He, (Jesus) did not do mighty works because of their unbelief." Jesus mentioned faith throughout the nine stories, giving evidence that the ones who were sick needed to believe and trust his healing power. Prayers with thanksgiving give us access to profound well-being.

Faith was not limited to those who were ill. It was the word from Jesus. To have faith in Christ was to believe who he was.

In the days Jesus walked the earth, faith in Christ was pertinent for salvation, so Jesus was satisfied with those who came to him in faith for both physical and spiritual restoration.

Physical healing is not the main focus of Jesus' healing work. The emphasis is shown in both the context and content that he was bringing comfort to those marginalized, providing relief to those burdened with the guilt of sin, reframing the community's understanding of the sabbath day, and showing the importance of the role of faith for healing and wholeness.

God sent Jesus for the benefit of the outcast. Jesus demonstrated his healing gifts to win people to his kingdom. He led those who were healed to believe by faith that their sins were forgiven. In my studies of the Greek version of the synoptic gospels, I conclude that healing is synonymous with salvation. Jesus never simply laid hands on people who sought healing. In some accounts, he did nothing physically, as people reached out to touch him. That was how the woman suffering from excessive bleeding was healed. (Mark 5:25-34) Jesus merely touched the hand of Peter's mother-in-law to cure of the fever. He touched the eyes of the blind. In Luke 7:14, we are told that Jesus touched the bier of a dead man being carried to his funeral. This man was raised from the dead. He used dirt and his own saliva on the tongue of a man with a speech impediment and on the eyes of a blind man. Not only in the synoptics but in John 9:1-15, we find Jesus making a mud paste out of his saliva and the ground and spread it out on a man's eyes to heal his blindness. In every one of these healings, he wanted those healings to connect with faith. This proved the ill were healed by not only his presence, but their personal faith was vital.

Jesus' healing word helps us to construct a healing place in our pandemic fears of today. We can and do not desire to have any status as a messiah, we can consider why healing was so much of our savior's life. So as Christ can heal, we might expect that his disciples both during this time or afterward would have the gift of healing. The methods might be similar to what Jesus was doing. Faith in the healer would be important, but healing is a small speck in our faith ministry. Final and ultimate healing is in him.

We discover the healing power of the apostles in the Acts. Jesus expected his disciples to heal. Besides preaching the Good News, they were to "cure the sick, raise the dead, cleanse the lepers, cast out demons." With God's blessing they were to do the same healing as Jesus. Read Matthew 17:14-20. By their faith and belief in Jesus disciples are empowered to heal. They used many of the same methods that Jesus used. For an example, the apostle Paul heals a paralytic after seeing that he possessed the faith to be healed. (Acts 14:9) Faith continues to bring physical healing. The main element in these processes is intimate prayer. Unrestrained delight comes at rare moments. Those negative events from minor irritations to major tragedies are part of every life. Prayer says grace for all the occasions. The joy of the Lord is strength to follow the inklings that point us to God's deepest yearnings. When Jesus spoke to his disciples before his death, he offered them his body and blood as gifts to cope with anything. He gave them both his joy and his pain.

In formal counseling and praying with people living with addictions, we begin twelve step centered work with the first step. They acknowledge existence of a Higher Power. Of course, they are given the freedom to define that term. With skeptics, I ask them to tell me what their conception and image of God is. We realize that God surpasses understanding. We are made aware of tributes of God's existence that we experience. Connecting with God on a regular and consistent basis in the building block to healing. In a real sense Christ finds a way to enter our lives through prayer. Choose a condition that you or somebody else has that you want to be healed and made whole.

"Thy will be done" are excellent words for keeping sanity in the world where we do not have the power to call the shots. Even in a pandemic or nuclear war, we can find strength in faith. Faith in a healing God is the key to opening up to experiencing God. We are witnesses to healing of others and ourselves. A complete view of healing requires us to look at suffering. Only then can we join the dream of God and appreciate the healing mission of Christ. The encounter with serious and pandemic leads to a predictable process within those who suffer. Some deny the illness, becoming angry. They become depressed and bitter. Prayer is the way of keeping in balance the desire to be healed and the need to admit that it is all out of our hands.

Feeling more connected in prayers for others. Healing prayers take us deeper. We are far beyond our personal concerns. Being involved and creating a life of healing is the willingness to try. We become willing to pray in expectation that healing will happen. Read John 16:23-24 and Luke 11:9-13. Ask and expect a blessing. I have felt a warm current of healing" flowing from a healer to a sick person. To heal and be healed, we search for a healing place with people whose physical contact is encouraged. The social environment may prevent healing. It takes a willingness to change, added to a strong desire to pray frequently and join others to praying, and the likelihood is that prayer will have a positive result.

The joy of salvation comes in the presence of the Holy Spirit. My soul felt the joy. Those who have joined me in prayer were committed and genuine. God always appears in such a gathering. I pray that my readers will seek the healing you need. In those intimate times, tell God about the brokenness you feel. Be open to God's willingness to heal, to give you ultimate peace and healing by the Great Physician. After my brother David died, the family benefited from hearing of David's wisdom and courage as he faced illness and death.

Nothing was wasted in David's years of chronic illness. After writing *Joy Comes in the Mourning: Love Is Forever,* I have shared that with all my soul, I know he is with Jesus, leaping and running, and exploring the place for eternity. No more need of a wheelchair or expensive medicine, he is unhampered by those disabilities that limited his life journey on earth. He is rejoicing in heaven, where God will wipe away all tears and "death will be no more; mourning and crying and pain will be no more, for the first things have passed away." (Revelation 20:4)

Bibliography

Bouyer, Louis. *The Spirituality of the New Testament and the Fathers.* New York: Seabury Press, 1983.

Brueggeman, Walter. *Praying the Psalms.* Winona, Minnesota: Saint Mary's Press, 1999.

Buttrick, George. *Prayer.* New York, Abingdon Press, 1962.

Clark, Connie, and Dale Matthews. *The Faith Factor.* New York: Viking Press, 1998.

DeLeon, Roy. *Praying with the Body: Bring the Psalms to Life.* Brewster, Massachusetts: Paraclete Press, 2009.

De'Arcy, Paula. *Crossing the Threshold: Crossing the Inner Barrier to Deeper Love.* New York: Crossroad, 2006.

Dorsey, Larry. *Healing Words: The Power of Prayer and the Practice of Medicine.* San Francisco: Harper and Row, 1993.

Edwards, Tilden. *Living in the Presence.* New York: Harper Collins, 1996.

Fosdick, Harry Emerson. *The Meaning of Prayer.* New York: Association Press, 1915.

Foster, Richard. *Prayer: Finding the Heart's True Home.* San Francisco: Harper/Collins, 1992.

Gilman, Cheryl. *Doing Work You Love to Do: Discovering Your Purpose and Realizing Your Dreams.* New York: Barnes and Noble Books, 1998.

Griffin, Emile. *The Experience of Prayer.* San Francisco: Harper and Row, 1984.

Guyon, Madame. *The Life of Prayer and the Way to God.* Goleta, California: Christian Spirituality Books, 1985.

Hays, Edward. *Prayers for the Domestic Church.* Greenwich, Connecticut: Forest of Peace Books, Inc., 1990

Indermark, John. *Traveling the Prayer Paths of Jesus.* Nashville: Upper Room Books, 1976.

Jones, Gregory. *Embodying Forgiveness: A Theological Analysis.* Grand Rapids, Michigan: William B. Eerdmans Publishing Company, 1995

Kierkegaard, Soren. *The Journals of Soren Kierkegaard, edited by Alexander Dru.* New York: Harper and Brothers, 1959.

Killinger, John. *Beginning Prayer.* Nashville: Upper Room Books, 2012.

Killinger, John. *Bread for the Wilderness, Wine for the Journey.* Waco, Texas Word Books, 1976.

Koenig. *The Healing Power of Faith.* New York Simon and Schuster, 1999.

Lewis, Gene, and David Stevens. *Jesus, M.D.,* Grand Rapids, Michigan: Zondervan Publishing House, 2004.

Luks, Allan, and Peggy Payne. *The Healing Power of Doing Good: The Health and Spiritual Benefits of Helping Others.* New York: Fawcett Columbine Books, 1994.

McReynolds, James. *Alcohol: America's Number One Drug Problem*. Nashville: Broadman Press, 1975.

McReynolds, James. *Dancing with Bipolar Bears: Living in Joy Despite Illness*. New York: Harper/ Collins, 2003.

McReynolds, James. *Dancing with God: A Theology of Joy*, 2016.

McReynolds, James. *Joy Comes in the Mourning: Love Is Forever*. Cleveland, Tennessee: Parson's Porch Books, 2020.

McReynolds, James. *Passionate Joy: Building a Wealth of Joy in a World Starved for Love*. New York, Shanghai: iUniverse, 2006.

McReynolds, James. *The Silence of the Church: The Spiritual Struggle with Sexuality*. Cleveland, Tennessee: Parson's Porch Books, 2017.

McReynolds, James. *The Spirituality of Joy*. Cleveland, Tennessee: Parson's Porch Books, 2011.

McReynolds, James. *Spirit of Joy Church*. Cleveland Tennessee: Parson's Porch Books, 2019.

McReynolds, James. *The Joy of Preaching: Encountering Jesus Through the Word of God*. Cleveland, Tennessee: Parson's Porch Books, 2013.

McReynolds, James. *Visionquest of Joy: The Least Discussed Human Emotion*. Bryn Mawr, Pennsylvania: Dorrance and Company, Incorporated, 1988.

Ornish, Dean. *Love and Survival: Eight Pathways to Intimacy and Health*. New York: Harper/Perennial, 1999.

Ornish, Dean. *Love and Survival: The Scientific Basis for the Healing Power of Intimacy*. New York: Harper/Collins, 1998.

Reeve, Christopher. *Nothing Is Impossible: Reflections on a New Life*. New York: Random House, 2005.

Ryan, Thomas. *Prayer of Heart and Body: Reclaiming the Body in Christian Spirituality*. Mahwah, New Jersey: Paulist Press, 2006.

Simmons, Henry C., and Jane Wilson. *Soulful Aging: Ministry Through the Stages of Adulthood*. Macon, Georgia: Smyth & Helwys Publishing Company, 2002.

Storms, S.C. *Healing and Holiness: A Biblical Response to the Faith-Healing Phenomenon*. Phillipsburg, New Jersey: Presbyterian and Reformed Publishing, 2006.

Swanson, Kenneth. *Uncommon Prayer: Approaching Intimacy with God*. New York: Ballentine, 1987.

Taylor, Scott. *Seasons of Prayer*. Cleveland, Tennessee: Parson's Porch Books, 2020.

Tournier, Paul. *The Healing of Persons*. New York: Harper and Row, Publishers, 1965.

Trueblood, Elton. *The Common Ventures of Life*. New York: Harper and Row, 1965.

Willard, Dallas. *The Spirit of the Disciplines*. San Francisco: Harper and Row, 1988.

Wooden, John with Steve Jamison. *Wooden: A Lifetime of Observations and Reflections on and Off the Court*. Lincolnwood, Illinois: Contemporary Books, 1997.

About the Author

Dr. James McReynolds is a minister concerned about prayer and the spiritual life. His many books on spirituality and joy have this focus. In his years of ministry, he has used a dialogue of prayer and action. Seldom has the intimacy with God in prayer been so dramatically realized and expressed in the life and writings of one person.

His writing is easy to read and thought-provoking. Anchored in the Bible, he has an irresistible understanding of prayer. When he was a student at Carson- Newman College, his English teacher got him in touch with Dr. Charles Trentham, pastor of the First Baptist Church in Knoxville, Tennessee where he served as student minister of prayer for four years.

James has often been asked to pray with people who are sick, grieving, and suffering losses. Along with his church ministries, he has served as a hospital, college, and mental health chaplain. He has served in impossible leadership roles and is listed in Who's Who in World. Jim served as public relations specialist for the Sunday School Board of the Southern Baptist Convention and for the Missouri Department of Mental Health. He is a retired elder in the United Methodist Church. He maintains standing as an ordained minister in the Christian Church (Disciples of Christ) in the United States and Canada.

His calling has been revealed as that of a communicator through preaching, teaching, writing, radio and television, pastoral psychotherapy, newsletters, blogs, prayer, and innovative ways to share the joy he has lived with the world.